Images of War

Images of War

World War One

A photographic record of
New Zealanders at war 1914–1918

GLYN HARPER

AND QUEEN ELIZABETH II ARMY MEMORIAL MUSEUM

HarperCollinsPublishers

National Library of New Zealand Cataloguing-in-Publication Data

Harper, Glyn, 1958-
Images of war : World War One / Glyn Harper and Queen
Elizabeth II Army Memorial Museum.
Includes bibliographical references.
ISBN 978-1-86950-676-6
1. World War 1914-1918—Pictorial works. I. Queen Elizabeth II
Army Memorial Museum. II. Title.
940.400222—dc 22

First published 2008
HarperCollins*Publishers (New Zealand) Limited*
P.O. Box 1, Shortland Street, Auckland

ISBN 978 1 86950 676 6

Cover design by Matt Stanton, HarperCollins Design Studio
Front and back cover images courtesy of National Army Museum
Waiouru, 2007-549 (front) and 1993-1032 H343 (back)
Typesetting by Springfield West

Printed by Everbest, China, on 128gsm Matt Art

Contents

Foreword

Go to any community in New Zealand and one will see the tremendous sacrifices recorded on war memorials and cenotaphs that this nation made to the war effort during that Great War of 1914–1918. You will see that no community was spared. Glyn Harper, in his *Images of War*, vividly portrays all those ingredients that have contributed to the making of New Zealand/Aotearoa into the nation it is today. As many commentators have recorded, it was the efforts of these brave men and women, who deployed from New Zealand on their 'big adventure' — a staggering 10 per cent of New Zealand's population, that contributed to this nation's coming of age.

Glyn has choreographed this pictorial edition so well. The photographs that he has presented tell a vivid story of the 'death and the pride' these brave warriors constantly faced in the 'desolation, death and mud' of the many battlefields into which they were thrown. Glyn has timed *Images of War* with military precision. Its release coincides with the 90th anniversary of the cessation of hostilities that were to end all wars and will provide every New Zealander with a superior photographic record of just what their forebears had to endure. Perhaps it is now timely for us all to take stock of their ordeals and sacrifices and for us to realise just how fortunate we all are as a consequence of their unselfish actions.

The National Army Museum is proud to have been a major contributor to this edition, ably supported by many photographs from private collections. The Museum prides itself in presenting the stories of these brave men and women, whether it is by our ever-changing exhibitions in the Museum or in association with military historians of the calibre of Glyn Harper.

Colonel Raymond J. Seymour (Rtd)
Director
National Army Museum, Waiouru

Acknowledgements

I wish to thank all those people who sent in photographs for this publication. The quality and range of images submitted was outstanding and my one regret is that I was not able to use them all.

The National Army Museum at Waiouru generously provided access to the magnificent collection of photographs stored there. I thank Lieutenant General (Rtd) Don McIver, Chair of the Museum's Executive Management Committee, and Colonel Raymond Seymour, the Museum's Director, for facilitating this access. I also wish to thank Colonel Seymour for writing the foreword to this book. In particular, I wish to acknowledge the work of Dolores Ho, the Museum's archivist, whose knowledge of the photographic collection is unsurpassed. Dolores helped me navigate my way through all of the First World War photographs in their collection and then devoted many hours to provide me with quality scans of the more than 1200 images I selected.

Dr Andrew Bamji, the curator of the Gillies Archives, Queen Mary's Hospital, Sidcup, Kent, provided open access to the Gillies material and was extraordinarily generous in his support of this project.

I wish to thank the team at HarperCollins (New Zealand) Publishers for commissioning me to undertake this project. I am particularly grateful to Lorain Day, who had the vision to initiate the book, and to Eva Chan, who tied it all together. I am grateful to Sue Page, who did an outstanding job of editing the manuscript; the book owes much to the care and diligence with which she undertook this task.

The secretary of Massey University's Centre for Defence Studies, Tania Lasenby, provided considerable support to this project. Tania assisted in the selection of images, scanned images and proofread most of this book. I am immensely grateful for her help and could not have met the publishing deadline without it. Similarly, Dr John Moremon, also of the Centre, greatly assisted with some of the more problematic electronic images.

Finally, I wish to acknowledge the support and encouragement of my wife, Susan Lemish, who assisted with the selection of photographs, typed up my handwritten captions, read all the first drafts and undertook the myriad other tasks necessary to bring this book to publication. Having a writer in the family is not easy, but Susan handles it with aplomb.

Glyn Harper
Palmerston North
August 2008

and reflective doctoral thesis as the 'democratization and commodification' of camera technology. She writes, 'Cameras required no special skill: it is a truism that anyone can point a camera, and ordinary soldiers avidly photographed and communicated their experiences.' The number of people who responded to the appeal and the quality of the photographs they produced certainly proves Callister's assertions.

Although the first war photograph ever taken was of American cavalry during the war with Mexico in 1846, it was not until the Crimean War, nearly a decade later, that war photography captured the public's imagination. When Roger Fenton, the first war photographer, travelled to the Crimea in 1855, the camera had been in existence for only 15 years. On his photographic expedition he was accompanied by 36 large cases of equipment that included five cameras of different sizes, over 700 glass plates on which the images were to be recorded, several chests of chemicals and a still for distilling water. The technique Fenton used to capture his images — the wet collodion process — allowed for the use of shorter exposure times, high definition images and the production of hundreds of images from the same negative. However, there was a downside to the process: when the glass plates were inserted into the camera they had to be coated with a light-sensitive solution. Once this dried, which usually took only 10 minutes, the plate was useless. This limitation meant that Fenton didn't often attempt to capture action shots, so war photography remained a static affair. The images produced were haunting, nonetheless.

By the time the First World War broke out, live action shots were possible, as lenses and celluloid film were both fast and portable enough to allow photographers to get close to — and capture — real combat action. Smaller cameras like the popular 'box Brownie' and the even more compact pocket models greatly assisted this process as anyone, provided they were undetected, could record combat action. There were still serious limitations to the technology. The cameras first taken to the war had a slow loading procedure: each exposure had to be loaded separately, the dark side removed and then the shutter released. This meant that the taking of combat action shots was still very much a hit-and-miss affair. This changed after October 1915, when Kodak produced what it called the 'greatest photographic invention in twenty years'. This was its small pocket camera, which enabled the user to record information on film at the time the picture was taken. In January 1916 Kodak began to market a version of this as 'The Soldiers' Kodak', promoting it as a way for soldiers to capture and record their war experiences. This small, portable camera proved immensely popular, with many soldiers enthusiastically embracing it. As the Australian historian Greg Kerr has noted, 'the Great War was arguably the photographic event of the century, and Australian soldiers compiled what is probably the most significant pool of amateur photographs from any war'. New Zealand soldiers were also enthusiastic users of this new photographic technology and captured thousands of images wherever the war took them. A small sample of their work appears in this book.

It was just as well that so many individual soldiers, often at considerable personal risk from both the enemy and their own military authorities, ignored the ban on cameras, as the warring governments, at least on the Allied side, were slow to appoint officially sanctioned war photographers. The British Expeditionary Force, under the influence of the Secretary of War, Lord Kitchener, who loathed the press, kept a very tight control over photographers and did not appoint any of its own until 1916, just prior to the battle of the Somme. Initially only two photographers, both army officers, were appointed to cover the entire Western Front. The New Zealand government waited until March 1917 to appoint its official photographer, H.E. Sanders, who was charged with recording the

New Zealanders' activities on the Western Front. Sanders, who had worked with the French pioneering cinema company Pathé Frères, was responsible for most of the 'H' series of photographs featured in this book. Sanders' 'H' series is the most extensive body of photographs depicting New Zealand soldiers on the Western Front. Sadly, by the time of Sanders' appointment, the Gallipoli campaign, the first battle of the Somme and several battles of the Sinai-Palestine campaign were over, so the opportunity to produce an official photographic record of these experiences was missed. Fortunately, some private photographs were taken at the time and these even appeared in public. The first newspaper photograph of the Gallipoli campaign appeared on the front cover of the *Auckland Weekly News* on 24 June 1915. It had been taken by Private R.B. Steele.

The most widely circulated photographs of the First World War, however, were taken by official photographers, who were controlled by the military authorities and subject to censorship. This led the leading military historian, John Keegan, to claim that 'by and large, the photograph archive of the Great War is extraordinarily dull and repetitive'. New Zealand's Sandy Callister made similar claims about the 'H' series of official photographs. She writes: 'Very few of these photographs [the 'H' series] give any impression of the nature of this war or the numbers dying.' Both judgements may be deemed harsh. There is something powerfully haunting and poignant about many of the photographs of the First World War. People relate well to visual images, especially still photographs that can be viewed again and again. Unlike the moving images of film and television, which appear in front of us only fleetingly, still images stamp themselves indelibly on our memories and become part of a collective consciousness. A good example of this is the series of photographs of British Expeditionary Force soldiers struggling through the mud and slime of Passchendaele; these images have almost attained an iconic status. Another photograph that falls into this category is the painful image of a long line of soldiers, temporarily blinded by gas, eyes bandaged, shuffling rearward for treatment. Outstanding images, when combined with the first-hand accounts of the combatants, bring the reader as close as it is possible to get to the realities of war. One only has to look at the pictures to know that fighting a war is a hard, brutal business that exacts a heavy toll on all involved. Those people who recorded these images were undoubtedly trying to portray the true nature of the war, and its human cost, although there was certainly a degree of self-censorship and personal selection involved.

A broad range of images has been selected for this book. All live action shots have been included, as they are extremely rare. Also included are images of battlefields, troops on the move or in static locations, wounded soldiers receiving treatment in makeshift regimental aid posts or established hospitals, and prisoners of war. Images of the hardware of war in action — rifles, artillery, tanks, machine guns firing, aircraft and battleships with a New Zealand connection — have been included. Images that record the daily life of the soldiers, whether in trenches, behind the lines or on leave, are featured too. Famous and infamous events and people are also portrayed. These include images of commanders, Victoria Cross winners, troublemakers and royal visits. Transport and logistics, crucial to any military combat, have not been ignored. A miscellaneous collection of images includes photographs of war animals, be they horses, mules, dogs, camels or birds; images of war graves; images from the Home Front; and the rather poignant images of soldiers leaving for the war and returning. It is hoped that these categories are broad enough to capture the essence of the New Zealand experience of the First World War.

There were several types of photograph that were not considered for inclusion in this book. First, if no information at all was known about a photograph, it was not included. Second, composite photographs, where photographs were altered or several negatives were combined to produce one good shot, were rejected. The Australian official photographer, Frank Hurley, was a master of this 'judicious manipulation', as he called it. He once used images from 12 different negatives to create a single photograph and regarded the final product, the famous image of Australian soldiers going 'over the top' at Zonnebeke, as one of his best creations. These composite photographs lack the realism and feeling of a natural image, and sometimes look more like a scene from a Hollywood movie than the real thing. Third, photographs that were obviously staged, especially if for propaganda purposes, were excluded.

The First World War has been described as 'the most important and far-reaching political and military event of the [twentieth] century'. There is little reason to doubt this statement. It is also widely acknowledged that the First World War was a pivotal event in New Zealand's history. What is surprising is that given its importance to this nation, so little has been written and published about that experience until very recently. Photographs of the New Zealand First World War experience are an important historical resource, and they have received scant attention to date. In contrast, the Australians produced *Photographic Record of the War* in 1923 as the last of their 12-volume official history. It was compiled by the far-sighted and influential General Editor of the series, Dr Charles Bean, who also provided the majority of the captions. The volume contained 753 illustrations and has been widely consulted ever since.

This book aims to redress the New Zealand imbalance some 90 years after the war ended, by presenting the first collection of photographs of New Zealanders in the First World War. It records a large slice of the New Zealand experience of this war, and reveals something of what it was like for the New Zealanders who were there. As Sandy Callister reminded the reader in the last line of her thesis: 'each image means that someone, at some point, took a photograph as a way of not forgetting'.

By preserving and examining these photographs, we do not forget either.

When the war came: New Zealand in 1914

The outbreak of a general European war in August 1914 came as a surprise to the government and people of New Zealand. News of the British declaration of war was received in Wellington on the morning of 5 August 1914. At 1 p.m. that day on the steps of the parliament buildings the Governor, Lord Liverpool, read a telegram advising that a state of war now existed between the British and German empires. The crowd of 15,000 people greeted the announcement with enthusiasm, cheering and then singing both the national anthem and 'Rule Britannia'. Other demonstrations of enthusiasm and support occurred throughout the country in the days that followed.

Though the war's immediate causes were little understood, most New Zealanders welcomed the opportunity to take part in it. There were several reasons for this. First, it was an opportunity for the small dominion to demonstrate its loyalty to Great Britain. Linked to this was the firm belief that the British Empire was sacrosanct. Historian Michael King has written of this unquestioning support for Britain:

> Implicit in all this was the conviction that the Empire as a whole would never put a foot wrong in matters of principle and foreign affairs, and that anyone who crossed Mother Britain was likely to be wrong and did so at their peril. A pamphlet popular in New Zealand at the time preached that the 'genius of

the British race is rooted in justice, truth, honour and consideration for the rights of others. The continued exercise of these principles has given virility to the race.'

Second, war was seen as a natural state of affairs that tested the quality, resolve and worth of a nation. In this great 'test' New Zealand wanted to play a full part. In addition to imperial sentiment and notions of social Darwinism, there was a strong degree of self interest. New Zealand's prosperity rested on its overseas markets, particularly in Britain, and it was the British Navy that provided the ultimate means of protecting New Zealand's trade routes. Anything that threatened Britain's security and the trade routes also threatened New Zealand's livelihood. There was also a feeling of moral outrage, stoked by the propaganda machines of the times, against the Central Powers' (Germany, Austria-Hungary, Turkey and Bulgaria) aggression towards smaller nations and its willingness to violate international law. The quest for world domination by Imperial Germany and Prussian militarism posed a fundamental challenge to the British Empire and this challenge had to be met. Neither the young men who were about to enlist in their thousands nor their families who supported them had any concept of the horrific, brutal nature that would characterise the modern, industrial war they were entering. Instead, they saw the war as a great adventure that offered them a chance of travel, glamour and glory. They knew that people were killed and wounded in wartime, but the sheer scale of casualties that would result from the First World War was unimagined in 1914, and moreover, few believed that it would ever happen to them.

When the United Kingdom declared war on Germany on 4 August the whole British Empire was also at war. It was, however, left up to the self-governing dominions to decide just how much support they would give to the war effort. All of them, New Zealand included, responded with an enthusiasm that far surpassed any obligation that could have been imposed from London. Promising to make any sacrifice that was necessary to fulfil 'the highest traditions of the great race and Empire to which we belong', the New Zealand government offered an Expeditionary Force of infantry, artillery and mounted rifles on the day it learned of the British declaration of war. The offer was accepted by the British government a week later. Volunteers were immediately called for, and the training camps set up around the country began to swell with the large influx of men who responded.

New Zealand was actually reasonably prepared for the event of war. In 1909 the Liberal Government of Sir Joseph Ward had passed a Defence Act that created a large Territorial Force, which was recruited through compulsory military training. Under the Act, boys between 15 and 18 years of age were required to serve in the cadet corps, with a minimum of 16 days' training. Between the ages of 18 and 25 years they served as Territorial Force soldiers, with a minimum requirement to complete 30 drills, 12 half-day parades and seven days in camp each year. The aim of the Act was to position the dominion so that it could provide around 100,000 well-armed, partially trained men for home defence and to allow the country to mobilise an effective military force in case of war. Suggestions for refinement made by Lord Kitchener during his visit in 1910 were implemented by Major General Alexander Godley, and this left New Zealand well-placed in 1914 to raise an Expeditionary Force for overseas service.

Prior to the sailing of what became the Main Body of the New Zealand Expeditionary Force, a 1400-strong scratch force, initially termed its 'Advance Guard', sailed for German-occupied Samoa on 15 August 1914. It did so at the request of the British government, which wanted the wireless station near Apia captured as 'a great and urgent Imperial service'. This operation was a considerable risk, as the force was ill-prepared and it was unknown if the German troops in Samoa would fight to defend this far-flung possession of Imperial Germany. The operation was successful, despite the haste with which it had been put together, and the New Zealand commander accepted the German surrender in Samoa on 29 August. It was the second German territory, after Togoland in West Africa, to be captured in the war.

Meanwhile, the Main Body, some 8500 men and 3800 horses, trained in their camps around New Zealand under the direction of Godley, who had been appointed as the General Officer Commanding the New Zealand Expeditionary Force. After a month's delay caused by a dispute with the British government over the lack of an adequate escort for the troopships, the Main Body of the New Zealand Expeditionary Force sailed from New Zealand on 16 October. According to Christopher Pugsley, this was the largest single body of men ever to leave New Zealand.

At Albany, Western Australia, the New Zealand troopships linked up with the Australian Imperial Force and their escorts, and sailed for the Mediterranean. The ships did not dock at Marseilles as most had expected. The entry of the Ottoman Empire into the war on the side of the Central Powers had altered the strategic situation, threatening Egypt and the vital Suez Canal. On 27 November, General Godley received a cable from the New Zealand government informing him that, 'Unforeseen circumstances decided Force train in Egypt and go front from there. Australians and New Zealand to form Corps under General Birdwood.' The Australian and New Zealand Army Corps consisted of the 1st Australian Division, commanded by Major General William Throsby Bridges, and the New Zealand and Australian Division, commanded by Godley. Not only did this arrangement initiate a new word in the English language, it meant that Australian and New Zealand military history would be forever intertwined.

The Anzacs arrived at Alexandria, Egypt on 3 December 1914. It was a world beyond the imagination of these soldier tourists. There, the Australians and New Zealanders experienced the pains and delights of a country they soon labelled as the land of 'shit, sand and syphilis'. Within two months New Zealand troops were in action for the first time in the war, defending the Suez Canal against an attack by the Turks. In only another two months they would be engaged in what is today one of the best-known ill-fated campaigns of the war — Gallipoli.

Lord Liverpool, with the Prime Minister William Massey at his right shoulder, reads the telegram from Britain announcing the declaration of war with Germany. This occurred on the steps of Parliament before a crowd of around 15,000 people. NATIONAL ARMY MUSEUM 1992-760

A show of hands in support of the resolution to continue the war until a satisfactory peace is obtained. Taken in Christchurch, date unknown. National Army Museum 1986-2086

Can't wait to go, Dunedin, 1914. Volunteers rushed to enlist in the months of 1914. Mark Febery

More volunteers from Dunedin off to the war. These are members of 18th Reinforcements marching through Dunedin on 29 June 1916. NATIONAL ARMY MUSEUM 2007-382

Clyde Waghorn rides to war in 1914 from his home 'Greendale' on the Banks Peninsula. LYNDALL WHITELOCK

Aerial view of Trentham Military Camp in November 1915. Trentham was the largest camp in New Zealand during the war, but camps like it were set up around New Zealand.
Matthew Pomeroy

New arrivals at Featherston Military Camp.
National Army Museum
1987-1733

The new arrivals about a week later.
National Army Museum
1987-1733

The new arrivals on a route march (LEFT) and at musketry practice on the 300 yards rifle range (RIGHT). All volunteers received plenty of both as part of their training.
NATIONAL ARMY MUSEUM 1987-1733, NATIONAL ARMY MUSEUM 1987-1733

Exhausted volunteers take a short break on a route march. They do not appear to be enjoying the experience.

Once the landing and formalities were over, New Zealand soldiers found many other activities to keep them occupied. Sliding down this waterfall was one way to have fun and stay cool. NATIONAL ARMY MUSEUM 1994-3348

This cartoon sums up the Samoan campaign, although it is doubtful the local Samoan community was as welcoming as the cartoon implies.
MATTHEW POMEROY

New Zealand soldiers march through the streets of Wellington on their way to the war.
NATIONAL ARMY MUSEUM 1986-2086, NATIONAL ARMY MUSEUM 1986-2086

*'Fearing no foe',
the soldiers of the
1st North Otago
Contingent set off
for the war.*
MATTHEW POMEROY

"THEY FEAR NO FOE"
1ST. NORTH OTAGO CONTINGENT OFF TO THE FRONT. No 3358.

*New Zealand
infantry preparing
to embark on the
Athenic in 1914.*
NATIONAL ARMY
MUSEUM 1992-742

*Members of the
Canterbury Yeoman
Cavalry lead their
mounts down the
Port Hills to the
Lyttelton Wharf.
They had travelled
with their horses
from the Addington
showground.*
NATIONAL ARMY
MUSEUM 1992-742

Canterbury Yeoman Cavalry troopers preparing to embark for Egypt. More than 3000 horses sailed with the Main Body of the New Zealand Expeditionary Force in 1914. NATIONAL ARMY MUSEUM 1998-960

Wellington bids farewell to a troopship. NATIONAL ARMY MUSEUM 1990-1717

The troopships were crowded, noisy and cramped, with little comfort for those who sailed on them.
NATIONAL ARMY MUSEUM 1993-1164

Lifeboat drill was conducted early in the voyage. NATIONAL ARMY MUSEUM 1993-1223

Off on the 'big adventure'. A troopship crowded with men leaves Wellington. National Army Museum 1986-2086

The last view of New Zealand for many on board. The Athenic *leaves Wellington Harbour.*
National Army Museum 1990-1717

Gallipoli

In mid-April 1915 the Australian and New Zealand troops boarded transports at Alexandria and sailed from Egypt to fight in their first major campaign of the war. It must be said that after the 'battle of the Wazza' on 2 April — Good Friday— when drunk and angry Anzacs ran amok in the red-light district of Cairo, the local Egyptians were probably glad to see them go.

While the Gallipoli campaign was not the first action of the war for New Zealand soldiers — they had been involved in the capture of German Samoa and in the defence of the Suez Canal in February 1915 — it was certainly the most significant of these early encounters. In many ways, and because it was the Anzacs' first real test in a clash of arms, the Gallipoli campaign has assumed a cultural significance out of all proportion to the military realities of the time. As we shall see later, the Western Front was the decisive theatre of war and was where the Anzacs truly made their mark in this war.

Initially, Gallipoli was meant to be a purely naval affair, beginning with an attempt to force open the Narrows, the gateway to Constantinople, on 19 February 1915. It was a dismal failure. Then, on 18 March, a great armada of 16 battleships, flotillas of cruisers and destroyers and hundreds of minesweepers set out for the Narrows. Great things were expected of this combined British-French fleet, but it also failed to penetrate the Turkish minefields and the Allies lost six capital ships in one day. The navy proved incapable of dealing with both the dense minefield laid across the Narrows and the Turkish artillery batteries, which were located on both sides of the straits. The only solution was to stage a landing to clear the shores.

The Mediterranean Expeditionary Force, led by General Sir Ian Hamilton, was given this formidable task. The Mediterranean Expeditionary Force consisted of the 29th, the Royal Naval, 1st Australian and Australian and New Zealand Divisions, and the *Corps expeditionnaire d'Orient*, French troops of about division strength. The Turkish forces numbered six weak divisions of about 84,000, which had to guard some 150 miles of coastline. General Hamilton had nowhere near enough troops for the size of the task ahead. Furthermore, the Turks knew a landing was imminent. As the Australians and New Zealanders were only partially trained and were inexperienced, they were given a subordinate role in the initial landings, a sideshow within a sideshow. After all, they were of doubtful quality. The Anzacs, as they had been designated, were to land to the north of Gaba Tepe, while the British and French carried out the main assault at Cape Helles.

The Australians and New Zealanders landed on the Gallipoli Peninsula in the early hours of 25 April 1915. For reasons never satisfactorily explained, they landed a mile north of the gentle beach that had been selected as their landing area. On all three sides of what became Anzac Cove tall cliffs dominated the area and overlooked the beach. The Australian and New Zealand soldiers who landed that morning knew they had to get as high and as deep as they could. Despite their best efforts, though, by late afternoon they had only penetrated to a depth of a mile and a half, still one mile short of the summit of the dominant Sari Bair ridge. They could get no further, thanks to the opposition that came from the Turkish defenders, organised by Mustapha Kemal, which, combined with the challenging terrain, left them exhausted.

After the initial landing and the abortive Second Battle of Krithia in early May which cost the New Zealand Brigade more than 800 men, an effort was made to consolidate and expand the lodgement achieved on the first day. This peaked in the major offensive of August 1915, in which the Anzac forces played a lead part. It was during this attack that the New Zealanders captured, and for a short time held, the Chunuk Bair ridge, the furthest point inland that the Allied forces penetrated. By September, though, with the failure of the August offensive, it was evident that the troops on Gallipoli were exhausted; evacuation was the only option. The troops were withdrawn three months later in what proved to be the most well-planned and well-executed operation of the whole campaign. It had lasted eight and a half months.

Gallipoli revealed the military potential and the natural talents of the New Zealand soldier, especially his ability to adapt to difficult circumstances. Natural ability could not compensate for failures in planning, leadership, logistics and administration, however, and no soldier in this war could afford to be committed to battle only half-trained. Nor could natural ability make up for a lack of men — and there were never enough men allocated to the Gallipoli campaign. There is no escaping the fact that the Gallipoli campaign was a serious defeat for the Allies. It was a costly failure and worse still, it had no significant effect on the war, apart from encouraging the Turks to fight on.

In Australia and New Zealand, much of the popular attention paid to the Gallipoli campaign has focused on the landing of 25 April. Yet New Zealand soldiers spent many months on the Gallipoli Peninsula. The dangers and hardships they endured there — the flies and lice and the disease they spread, the dreadful plight of the wounded, the harsh climate, the poor rations, the losses from snipers and bombs — made serving on Gallipoli a harrowing experience.

The Australian writer Les Carlyon has calculated that about one million men in total served on Gallipoli and between one-third and one-half of them became casualties. These are staggering losses. The Turks, who neither buried nor counted their dead, lost approximately 260,000 men killed, wounded or missing. The Allies lost around 140,000. One Allied division, the reliable and overworked 29th, lost its strength twice over. New Zealand casualty rates were also extraordinary and have recently been the subject of major revision by the historian Richard Stowers. Acknowledging that the precise figures will never be known, after painstaking analysis Stowers estimated that 13,977 New Zealanders served on the peninsula and more than half, 7991, became casualties. Of these, 2779 New Zealanders were killed in action or died from accidents and disease. This figure is around 20 per cent of those who served and includes 55 pairs of brothers. Only 344 have known grave sites. Of the others, 252 were buried at sea, but the rest, more than 2000 men, have no known grave, many lying where they fell in action. Unfortunately for both Anzac nations, this was just the beginning of the long casualty lists that were to be an enduring feature of the war.

As so many commentators have noted, New Zealand lost more than just many of its soldiers at Gallipoli. It also lost its innocence. While this is true, New Zealand at the same time discovered something about itself, with the first stirrings of a national identity emerging from the fighting on that far-off peninsula in the Aegean Sea.

Men and horses disembark at Alexandria in December 1914.
NATIONAL ARMY MUSEUM 1993-1223,
NATIONAL ARMY MUSEUM 1993-1223

Foot inspection for New Zealand soldiers prior to heading to Gallipoli.
MATTHEW POMEROY

Part of the main New Zealand camp at Zeitoun in Egypt. NATIONAL ARMY MUSEUM 1991-587

New Zealand soldiers practise bayonet fighting at Zeitoun Camp. NATIONAL ARMY MUSEUM 2006-88

Part of the Wazza district damaged by rampaging Anzacs on Good Friday 1915. The cause of the riot was boredom and anger. The Anzac soldiers were angry at the poor quality of the beer and it was rumoured that the Egyptians urinated in it to make it go further. A virulent strain of venereal disease in the red-light district intensified the anger. In the inquiry that followed, each Anzac nation blamed the other for causing the disturbance.
National Army Museum 1990-1712, National Army Museum 1990-1712

Breakfast on the wharf at Alexandria prior to embarking for Gallipoli. National Army Museum 2001-215

New Zealand troops embark for their first major campaign of the war. NATIONAL ARMY MUSEUM 1992-1149

Members of the Auckland Battalion train for the landing at Port Mudros.
NATIONAL ARMY MUSEUM 1987-1647

Why the navy effort failed and a landing was necessary. A 9-inch gun at Kilid Bahr, Chanak. This photograph was taken in 1919.
NATIONAL ARMY MUSEUM 2007-553

New Zealand soldiers being towed towards Gallipoli.
NATIONAL ARMY MUSEUM
1987-1647

New Zealand soldiers caught 'betwixt ship and shore'.
NATIONAL ARMY MUSEUM
1992-1647

New Zealanders heading towards the Gallipoli shore.
NATIONAL ARMY MUSEUM
1991-321

New Zealand troops land on the shores of Gallipoli on 25 April 1915. NATIONAL ARMY MUSEUM 2001-215

A different view of New Zealand soldiers landing on Gallipoli. NATIONAL ARMY MUSEUM 2007-27

Two different, high-angle images of the New Zealanders at Gallipoli on 25 April 1915.
National Army Museum 2007-27, National Army Museum 2007-27

Exhausted men of the Auckland Battalion rest at the foot of the cliffs at Anzac Cove. NATIONAL ARMY MUSEUM 1987-1647

Towards the end of the day the small cove was crowded with Australian and New Zealand soldiers. NATIONAL ARMY MUSEUM 1992-1149

A view of V Beach on the day of the landing. NATIONAL ARMY MUSEUM 1991-321

Over the next few days, mountains of stores had to be unloaded at Anzac Cove. This continued until the Anzac soldiers were eventually evacuated from the peninsula. NATIONAL ARMY MUSEUM 2007-27

NATIONAL ARMY MUSEUM 1991-587

The Anzacs could not have been landed at a worse place. Instead of finding a gentle sloping plain, as they expected, the soldiers were landed at the base of steep, barren cliffs. The Turks soon occupied the vital high ground, leaving the Anzacs clinging to a shallow, crowded enclave. The following five images reveal the stark, inhospitable terrain of Anzac Cove. The first image, made from two photographs joined together, gives a wide-angle view from Anzac Cove to Plugges Plateau. National Army Museum 2006-88

National Army Museum 1993-1203

National Army Museum 1992-742

National Army Museum 1992-1153

The slopes of Walker's Ridge.
NATIONAL ARMY MUSEUM 1990-1712

The knife-edge spur known as the Sphinx.
NATIONAL ARMY MUSEUM 1992-776

The slopes above Anzac Cove were soon crowded with men. This is the road up to Walker's Ridge.
ALLAN COMRIE

Dugout shelters in the cliffs above Anzac Cove.
NATIONAL ARMY MUSEUM 1992-742

Courtney's Post. ALLAN COMRIE

The Nelson Company of the Canterbury Battalion at the foot of Walker's Ridge on 25 April 1915.
NATIONAL ARMY MUSEUM 1992-776

The Auckland Battalion digs in on the left flank of the New Zealand position. NATIONAL ARMY MUSEUM 1987-1647

A shell bursting on the slopes of Gallipoli. NATIONAL ARMY MUSEUM 2001-215

Live action images during the war are rare. This is one of them. A New Zealand soldier fires his rifle from a hastily constructed trench. NATIONAL ARMY MUSEUM 2001-215

This is unlikely to be a live action shot. There is very little protection for those firing, while the officer is totally exposed. However, it could be an actual action shot, and if it is, reveals the inexperience of the New Zealanders, as the image was taken early in the campaign. NATIONAL ARMY MUSEUM 1992-1149

A New Zealand soldier alert and ready in the trenches at Pope's Hill. NATIONAL ARMY MUSEUM 1992-759

The invention of the periscope rifle made observation and firing on the enemy easier and safer. NATIONAL ARMY MUSEUM 2007-550

The outstanding New Zealand Commanding Officer of the campaign was William Malone, who had command of the Wellington Battalion. Malone's battalion captured the key position of Chunuk Bair in August, but he was killed defending the position against counterattacks. He was a major when this photograph was taken.
NATIONAL ARMY MUSEUM 1992-756

New Zealand soldiers trying to find out what is happening on the other side of the hill.
NATIONAL ARMY MUSEUM 1993-1293

Originally annotated 'Ready', this image shows New Zealanders putting the periscope rifle to good use.
NATIONAL ARMY MUSEUM 2007-550

A fire-step in the Anzac front line early in the campaign. National Army Museum 2007-550

The strain showing on his face, a soldier readies a trench mortar for firing. National Army Museum 1990-1712

A machine-gun sniper. The position has the appearance of being hastily constructed, especially when compared with the next image. NATIONAL ARMY MUSEUM 2007-550

Ross Cardno uses a machine gun in a well-constructed defensive position. NATIONAL ARMY MUSEUM 2001-215

A bunkered supply depot on the beach of Anzac Cove.
NATIONAL ARMY MUSEUM 1992-742

Inside a cramped Gallipoli dugout.
NATIONAL ARMY MUSEUM 1992-759

A precious water point at Anzac Cove. All water had to be brought ashore by barge with the other supplies. It was always in short supply. NATIONAL ARMY MUSEUM 2007-550

Unloading mules at the Narrows.
NATIONAL ARMY MUSEUM 1992-1153

This is the way most supplies reached the frontline soldiers, including food and water. In this image the donkeys are carrying ammunition. NATIONAL ARMY MUSEUM 2006-88

The Patan Mule Corps was used to resupply the men fighting on the peninsula.
NATIONAL ARMY MUSEUM 1992-742

New Zealand soldiers digging in at Cape Helles in May 1915. NATIONAL ARMY MUSEUM 1992-776

Members of the Anzac Battalion mix with French soldiers at Cape Helles. NATIONAL ARMY MUSEUM 1987-1647

One of the few escapes from the dreadful conditions on the peninsula. These New Zealanders are bathing at Cape Helles, rather than at Anzac Cove. They still needed to be vigilant, as the Turks occasionally shelled the water just off the beaches. NATIONAL ARMY MUSEUM 1992-1149

The Quartermaster of the 15th Company Auckland Battalion is being sentenced for seeking solace from the war. In the shadow of Walker's Ridge, an Orderly Room is being conducted and the Quartermaster is being tried for stealing the men's rum ration.
SUSAN PRICE

The aftermath of a Turkish attack. The exact location of this trench is unknown.
NATIONAL ARMY MUSEUM 1992-760

Men rest and relax on the heights of Gaba Tepe during a brief armistice. The armistice was used to bury the dead of both sides. The Turkish trenches are only 30 yards away from this position. MATTHEW POMEROY

Turkish prisoners of war at Gallipoli do not seem too concerned about their fate.
NATIONAL ARMY MUSEUM 1988-1753

Cremating enemy dead on Gallipoli.
NATIONAL ARMY MUSEUM 1991-321

New Zealand soldiers tend to a comrade's grave. Very few of the New Zealanders killed on Gallipoli have a known grave. NATIONAL ARMY MUSEUM 2007-27

NATIONAL ARMY MUSEUM 2007-550

Carrying a wounded soldier along the beach at Anzac Cove. Soldiers in the background are having their daily wash.
NATIONAL ARMY MUSEUM 1992-742

The plight of the wounded at Anzac Cove was truly pitiful. Wounded soldiers often had to endure days of waiting, then several sets of rough handling until they reached the comfort of a hospital ship. Here, a barge carrying sick and wounded New Zealanders pulls alongside the hospital ship Maheno.
NATIONAL ARMY MUSEUM 2007-550

Seriously wounded solders had to be hoisted aboard the hospital ship using a pulley and chain.
ALLAN COMRIE

Walking wounded and sick being transferred to a captured enemy vessel, which has been renamed the Huntsgreen *and is being used as a hospital ship.*
NATIONAL ARMY MUSEUM 2007-550

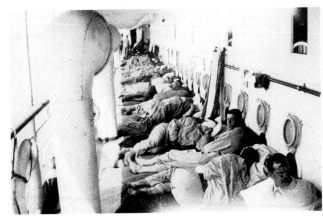

Wounded soldiers on the deck of the Dunluce Castle. MATTHEW POMEROY

Some New Zealand walking wounded from Gallipoli. NATIONAL ARMY MUSEUM 1991-587

Turkish prisoners on the island of Mudros. NATIONAL ARMY MUSEUM 2006-88

The strain shows clearly on the faces of these New Zealanders in the trenches of Gallipoli, despite their attempts to smile. The names are given as Hall-Jones, G. Brow, Fisher and Olsen, although the order in which they appear is not clear.
NATIONAL ARMY MUSEUM 1987-1647

Men of the Auckland Battalion in the frontline trenches at Gallipoli.
NATIONAL ARMY MUSEUM 1987-1647

No. 2 Outpost Trench. The close-cropped hair was common on Gallipoli. It enabled soldiers to better control lice, or 'chats' as they were known. NATIONAL ARMY MUSEUM 1991-587

Trench-digging was
exhausting work.
NATIONAL ARMY
MUSEUM 1992-1149

The Bartlett brothers look incredibly weary in September 1915.
NATIONAL ARMY MUSEUM 1992-757

Using a trench periscope, a soldier
keeps a wary eye on the Turkish lines.
NATIONAL ARMY MUSEUM 1987-1647

The Parcel Branch of the New Zealand Expeditionary Force Postal Unit. Getting mail through as regularly as possible was vital to the morale of soldiers. NATIONAL ARMY MUSEUM 2006-88

A New Zealand doctor does his 'rounds' in the trenches. NATIONAL ARMY MUSEUM 1992-742

The water point at Shrapnel Gully allowed these soldiers to have a quick wash. NATIONAL ARMY MUSEUM 1992-759

A bunkered headquarters at Anzac Cove.
NATIONAL ARMY MUSEUM 1992-742

Two soldiers enjoy a meal. Most meals consisted of tinned bully beef, hard tack biscuits and apricot jam. Tea was always welcome, almost as much as the rum ration. NATIONAL ARMY MUSEUM 1992-742

New Zealand soldiers pose around an unexploded Turkish shell, nicknamed a 'Jack Johnson'. It was named after a particularly large American boxer.
NATIONAL ARMY MUSEUM 2001-215

A soldier maintains the gas guard at Gallipoli. Despite the precaution, gas was not used during the campaign. NATIONAL ARMY MUSEUM 2007-550

During the war, animals provided the New Zealand soldiers with some solace from the dreadful conditions they were facing. Gallipoli was no exception. This photograph carried the apt annotation: 'A precious pet'. NATIONAL ARMY MUSEUM 2007-550

A carved stone marks the communal grave of six Canterbury mounted riflemen, killed at Walden's Point on 6 August 1915. NEIL BRUERE

Walden's Point, captured by the New Zealand Mounted Rifles with heavy losses on the evening of 6 August 1915. NEIL BRUERE

At the Somme in 1916 the New Zealand Division passed its first great test of the war, and in doing so established a formidable reputation. This success came at a very high price. It would be many months before the New Zealand Division would be able to be committed to another major action.

The first man to command a New Zealand Division. The newly promoted Major General Andrew Russell on board the SS Arawa *and about to sail for France.* NATIONAL ARMY MUSEUM 1992-773

New Zealand troops embark on the SS Arawa *bound for France.* NATIONAL ARMY MUSEUM 1992-773

New Zealand troops in France march towards the front. NATIONAL ARMY MUSEUM 2007-549

The King and senior British officers visit the New Zealand Division. NATIONAL ARMY MUSEUM 2007-549

The town of Armentières, with the tower of the Hotel de Ville on the right. This photograph was taken through a shell hole in a local school. NATIONAL ARMY MUSEUM 2007-183

Part of the town of Armentières. Both photographs were taken in July 1916, the morning after an artillery bombardment. NATIONAL ARMY MUSEUM 1991-2558, NATIONAL ARMY MUSEUM 2007-183

The ruins of Armentières. NATIONAL ARMY MUSEUM 1991-321

The remains of a cookhouse at Armentières after it took two direct hits.
NATIONAL ARMY MUSEUM 1990-1712

An observation post in the ruins of Armentières. Two observers of the 4th Battalion, New Zealand Rifle Brigade are on duty and they take turns using the telescope.
NATIONAL ARMY MUSEUM 1991-2558

NATIONAL ARMY MUSEUM 1991-2558

New Zealand soldiers on a daylight bombing party. Operating in daylight like this was incredibly risky; most bombing parties and raids were done at night. NATIONAL ARMY MUSEUM 1992-773

*French civilians return to the ruins of their homes,
searching for anything that remains.*
National Army Museum 1991-584

*A French woman washes her clothes in all that
remains of her home.*
National Army Museum 1992-773

Wearing their best clothes and carrying their most valuable possessions, French refugees leave Armentières.
National Army Museum 2007-549

The lonely grave of a New Zealand soldier in the front line at Armentières. NATIONAL ARMY MUSEUM 1991-2558

The front line at Armentières, showing a soldier ready with a sniperscope rifle. Dugouts are on the left in the parados (rear side of the trench).
NATIONAL ARMY MUSEUM 1991-2558

The front line at Armentières. This is Chards Farm salient; the sandbags in the foreground are covering gas cylinders. NATIONAL ARMY MUSEUM 2007-183

Searching for dead soldiers at Armentières after a heavy bombardment. NATIONAL ARMY MUSEUM 1991-2558

The gas officer ready to release his deadly chemical cocktail at Chards Farm salient. NATIONAL ARMY MUSEUM 2007-183

Both sides used gas extensively during the war. When this gas alarm in the trenches was rung, soldiers immediately had to don gas masks and wear them until the all-clear was given. NATIONAL ARMY MUSEUM 2007-183

Communication trenches near Armentières. NATIONAL ARMY MUSEUM 2007-183, NATIONAL ARMY MUSEUM 2007-183

A spell for some riflemen in a reserve trench at Armentières. NATIONAL ARMY MUSEUM 1991-2558

Officers' dugout in the close support line at Chards Farm salient. Lieutenant J. Price of the Rifle Brigade has had his reading interrupted.
NATIONAL ARMY MUSEUM 2007-183

Lieutenant G. Mawley takes a pot-shot at some rats from the window of his dugout.
NATIONAL ARMY MUSEUM 2007-183

Two officers of the 4th Battalion, New Zealand Rifle Brigade relaxing in reserve trenches at Armentières. They are Lieutenant G. Mawley and Lieutenant Kenneth Clayton.

Lieutenant Mawley moves cautiously through no-man's-land at Armentières.

A Lewis gun section of the 4th Battalion, New Zealand Rifle Brigade in the front line at Armentières.

A cup of tea in the trenches. Note the handy location of the rum jars. NATIONAL ARMY MUSEUM 1991-2558

A frontline firing bay at Armentières, with dugouts in the parapets. NATIONAL ARMY MUSEUM 1991-2558

The Somme battlefield across which the New Zealand Division had to advance. It was gently sloping farmland, but the Germans held the high ground. National Army Museum 1990-1712

National Army Museum 1990-1712

National Army Museum 1990-1712

Part of the Somme battlefield. The ruins of the village of Flers. NATIONAL ARMY MUSEUM 1990-1712

The battlefield around Flers village. NATIONAL ARMY MUSEUM 1990-1712

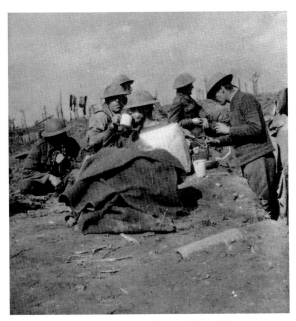

New Zealand gunners snatch a quick meal on the Somme battlefield. NATIONAL ARMY MUSEUM 1990-1712

Some gunners pose with their camouflaged gun. NATIONAL ARMY MUSEUM 1999-1961

The remains of an 18-pounder gun that has received a direct hit. NATIONAL ARMY MUSEUM 1999-1961

New Zealand gunners prepare for action on the Somme. NATIONAL ARMY MUSEUM 1990-1712

A New Zealand gun has been badly damaged by German counterbattery fire. NATIONAL ARMY MUSEUM 1990-1712

A New Zealand 18-pounder at full recoil after firing. NATIONAL ARMY MUSEUM 1992-773

A medic collects an identification disc from a dead soldier. National Army Museum 1991-321

The annotation to this photograph reads: 'Desolation, death and mud'. By the end of their part in the Somme battle, the New Zealanders had certainly had their share of all three. National Army Museum 1991-321

The Western Front: France and Belgium 1917

The year 1917 was the worst of the war for the Allies. With a few exceptions it was a year of disaster and defeat on the battlefields, and massive losses were incurred. For the French it was also a time of full-scale mutiny in their armies. Russia, after enduring defeat on the battlefield and revolutions at home, was knocked out of the war by the year's end. The United Kingdom's military misfortunes were compounded as the island nation was slowly driven to starvation by unrestricted submarine warfare. After three long years of attrition, with the end nowhere in sight, the warring nations were growing weary and nearing exhaustion.

For New Zealand, 1917 was a long, hard year — and the only full year of service for the New Zealand Division on the Western Front. Brought up to full strength after their experience on the Somme and having spent considerable time training the new arrivals, the New Zealanders undertook their first large offensive in the middle of the year. On the morning of 7 June 1917 the soldiers from nine divisions of the British Expeditionary Force's Second Army stormed the Messines Ridge in the Ypres salient, with the New Zealanders and Australians playing key roles. The soldiers' tasks had been made much easier by the meticulous planning of General Sir Herbert Plumer and the Second Army Staff, planning that included the successful detonation of 19 huge mines beneath the German frontline trenches. The New Zealand Division had been assigned the task of capturing Messines village and the success of the whole operation depended on them being able to take this objective quickly. The New Zealand attack at Messines went flawlessly and, apart from a later attack in October, it was the only high point the New Zealanders were to experience in 1917.

The New Zealanders missed the first four battles that make up the Third Ypres offensive, but they returned to the Ypres salient in October to take part in two great set-piece attacks. The first, launched on 4 October 1917, was a stunning success. All the allocated objectives were easily taken although, at 25 per cent, the casualty rate was heavy. This action was labelled the battle of Broodseinde. The next attack, made just over a week later, on 12 October, was a tragic failure and remains New Zealand's worst-ever military disaster. During this First Battle of Passchendaele, as it came to be known, more New Zealanders were killed or maimed on a single morning than on any other day since the European settlement of New Zealand. Some 846 New Zealand soldiers were killed and a further 3000 were wounded in the space of a few short hours that fateful morning. It was indeed a black day for New Zealand.

In early December came another failed attack, this time at the Polderhoek Chateau, and made by units from the 2nd New Zealand Infantry Brigade. This minor action, a costly failure for the two battalions involved, captured some ground, but the main objective eluded the weary New Zealanders.

These disasters were aggravated by the weather of 1917. With a late spring, a very short summer, the heaviest rainfall in 75 years and one of the worst winters on record, it was little wonder that New Zealand and other Allied troops had trouble making headway, as battlegrounds quickly became quagmires. From 12 October, morale in the New Zealand Division plummeted. The end of 1917 was truly 'a winter of discontent' and the spirit of the New Zealand Division hit the depths of despair. Every division has its breaking point and the New Zealanders in 1917 very nearly reached the limits of their endurance.

The losses associated with the major actions of 1917 were very heavy: 6500 at Messines, 7500 for the two actions at Passchendaele, followed by more than 3000 for the winter months of 1917–18. Every one of these was a person with a family, with friends, and with hopes of a return to New Zealand and a better life there.

Other armies mutinied or fell apart in 1917, but there was never any danger of this occurring in the British Expeditionary Force, which is a huge tribute to the courage and tenacity of all of its soldiers. No matter how bleak the year, the New Zealand soldier never lost his sense of humour, although it occasionally became very dark. In fact, a sense of humour, like mateship, national pride and self-respect, was one of the vital coping mechanisms that helped sustain New Zealand soldiers and others through the dreadful conditions that year. In 1917, these coping mechanisms were stretched to their limits, as conditions on the Western Front deteriorated to an all-time low.

Prior to the New Zealand Division taking part in the battle of Messines in mid-1917, the men went through a period of intensive training. Here, New Zealand NCOs hone their bayonet skills using a device known as a blot stick. NATIONAL ARMY MUSEUM 1999-111 H313

A delegation from New Zealand, including the Prime Minister, William Massey, stands on the lip of one of the mine craters at Messines.
NATIONAL ARMY MUSEUM 1991-321

Brigadier Fulton, commander of the New Zealand Rifle Brigade, looking over the area his brigade would attack at Messines.
NATIONAL ARMY MUSEUM 1993-1032 H41

New Zealand artillery concealed in a wood near Messines. NATIONAL ARMY MUSEUM 1993-1032 H54

LEFT: *New Zealand guns ready for action. As General Russell later stated, the battle was won by the sheer weight of metal hurled at the enemy and by the spirit of the men.* NATIONAL ARMY MUSEUM 1993-1032 H58

BELOW: *A New Zealand howitzer fires in the opening barrage of the Messines battle.*
NATIONAL ARMY MUSEUM 1993-1032 H53

BOTTOM: *New Zealand artillery shells score direct hits on Messines village.*
NATIONAL ARMY MUSEUM 1993-1032 H65

A partially concealed 6-inch howitzer.
NATIONAL ARMY MUSEUM 1999-1961

*Danger for the gunners. The same gun after
an artillery shell exploded in the barrel.*
NATIONAL ARMY MUSEUM 1999-1961

A New Zealand chaplain celebrating Holy Communion on the edge of the battlefield.
NATIONAL ARMY MUSEUM 1993-1032 H69

New Zealand soldiers on Messines Ridge. Note the shells bursting in the background.
National Army Museum 1993-1031 H815

A British tank stranded on Messines Ridge.
Louise Marsh

Dead German soldiers; their position has been overrun.
National Army Museum
1992-745 D775

Another position immediately after its capture.
National Army Museum
1990-106

Part of the German positions on Messines Ridge.
NATIONAL ARMY MUSEUM
1987-2176

The remains of a German concrete bunker. Its walls were 44 centimetres thick.
NATIONAL ARMY MUSEUM
1993-1032 H66

Part of the ruins of Messines village.
NATIONAL ARMY MUSEUM
1993-1032 H67

A New Zealand advanced dressing station on Messines Ridge. NATIONAL ARMY MUSEUM 1993-1032 H62

A New Zealand stretcher-party carries a soldier wounded at Messines. Luckily, at Messines, the wounded did not have far to travel. NATIONAL ARMY MUSEUM 1993-1032 H60

This YMCA hut has received a direct hit but still continues to function.

New Zealand officers wander around the ruins of Ypres. By late 1917, New Zealand soldiers had become used to seeing death and destruction at very close range. Even so, the annihilation of the town of Ypres and the overpowering smell of death shocked most New Zealanders who experienced it.
NATIONAL ARMY MUSEUM 1990-1711 H307

New Zealand soldiers awed by the ruins of Ypres Cathedral. NATIONAL ARMY MUSEUM 1993-1032 H305

A New Zealand detail passes the ruins of the Cloth Hall at Ypres. NATIONAL ARMY MUSEUM 1997-21 H511

New Zealand gunner Victor Middlebrook poses by his 'bivvy' at Passchendaele. MATTHEW POMEROY

This New Zealand field gun has taken a direct hit from German counterbattery fire. MATTHEW POMEROY

New Zealand troops march to the front in the Ypres salient. This photograph was taken near Kansas Farm.
NATIONAL ARMY MUSEUM 1990-1711 H288

They marched past the ruins of villages. National Army Museum 1990-1714

When the roads ended, they marched over duckboards. This was designated the No. 6 Track.
National Army Museum 1990-1714

One of the most dangerous jobs in the war. A runner leaves the Company Headquarters with an important message. NATIONAL ARMY MUSEUM 1993-1032 H362

New Zealand stretcher-bearers at Ypres being shelled by the Germans. GILLIAN GASKELL

A New Zealand advanced dressing station set up at the ruins of a farmhouse on the Passchendaele battlefield.
BRENT AND PENNY CLOTHIER

A New Zealand ambulance hit by German artillery.
BRENT AND PENNY CLOTHIER

New Zealand soldiers assist a wounded German near Gravenstafel on 6 October 1917.
NATIONAL ARMY MUSEUM 1990-1714

German prisoners assist in carrying wounded. This was taken at Spree Farm, near Ypres, on 4 October 1917.
NATIONAL ARMY MUSEUM 1990-711 H287

New Zealand soldiers rest near the Wieltze Road. NATIONAL ARMY MUSEUM 1990-1711 H292

A German blockhouse in the Reserve Line just after its capture.
GILLIAN GASKELL

New Zealand soldiers rest in a relatively intact wood near Louvencourt. NATIONAL ARMY MUSEUM 1990-1711 H514

Conditions in the Ypres salient from early October 1917 were dreadful. They were as bad as it could possibly get on the Western Front. The next 20 photographs reveal something of the conditions the men endured in the Ypres salient during a period that has been called 'the slough of despond'. This is a famous image of duckboards, wire, soldiers and mud at Carter Point, taken on 23 October 1917. NATIONAL ARMY MUSEUM 1994-3346

The landscape near Jargon Crossroads, taken in December 1917. Note the two tanks stranded in the mud.
NATIONAL ARMY MUSEUM 1994-3346

The Ypres battlefield. NATIONAL ARMY MUSEUM 1991-32

An image of the battlefield at Passchendaele.
NATIONAL ARMY MUSEUM 2008-8

A well-named avenue in the salient. MATTHEW POMEROY

Bringing stores forward on a plank road. The margin for error was slight. NATIONAL ARMY MUSEUM 1992-773

A New Zealand soldier's home in the Flanders mud.
MATTHEW POMEROY

A famous Flanders image. The gunners try to free a field gun from the mud.
NATIONAL ARMY MUSEUM 1999-929

More often than not, horses were required to shift the guns.
NATIONAL ARMY MUSEUM 2002-7

But even the horses struggled.
NATIONAL ARMY MUSEUM 1999-929

Another animal in difficulties.
NATIONAL ARMY MUSEUM 1993-1032 H285

A mule carries eight rounds of field artillery, while its handler makes a vain attempt to stay dry. NATIONAL ARMY MUSEUM 1999-929

Two New Zealand soldiers contemplate the destruction and desolation of the Ypres battlefields.
NATIONAL ARMY MUSEUM 1992-773

The winter of 1917–18 was one of the coldest on record. The Flanders mud is covered with thick snow. NATIONAL ARMY MUSEUM 2005-749

Soldiers struggle wearily towards Ypres.
GILLIAN GASKELL

New Zealand soldiers seek shelter from the cold in the Ypres salient. NATIONAL ARMY MUSEUM 1990-1711 H394

Wintry conditions at the New Zealand headquarters — Chateau Segard, Dickelbusch.
NATIONAL ARMY MUSEUM 1997-21

New Zealand signallers battle the ice and mud at Ypres. At times the ice that formed in the shell craters was thick enough to walk across. NATIONAL ARMY MUSEUM 1991-321

Both sides fired millions of artillery shells during the Third Battle of Ypres. These are the shell casings fired by New Zealand gunners after a particularly busy period. NATIONAL ARMY MUSEUM 1991-321 C985

The anti-aircraft guard of the New Zealand Pioneer Battalion. The Lewis gun, with its 47-round drum, was not actually designed for this role. NATIONAL ARMY MUSEUM 1993-1031

New Zealand soldiers at the base camp in Étaples receive mail from home. Letters and newspapers were shared with friends. The mail from home was always welcomed. NATIONAL ARMY MUSEUM 1997-21

New Zealanders board the train near Ypres. They were greatly relieved to leave the Flanders region in early February 1918. NATIONAL ARMY MUSEUM 1999-1709 H279

The Western Front 1918

The heavy casualties of 1917, combined with a dwindling manpower pool, forced the British to reduce their divisions from 12 infantry battalions to nine at the beginning of 1918. Even then, most of their units remained under strength. While the Australians soon followed this reorganisation, the Canadians and New Zealanders did not. With its 12 infantry battalions at full strength, plus an additional three entrenching battalions formed from the rump of the disbanded 4th New Zealand Brigade, the New Zealand Division in 1918 was the strongest in the British Expeditionary Force. Backed by an adequate reinforcement pool in the United Kingdom, the New Zealand Division was able to maintain its strength throughout 1918. It was, in fact, the equivalent of a British Corps for all of that year.

The year 1918 was an important one for the Allied divisions on the Western Front, as the nature of the war changed irrevocably. It was to be the year of movement, mobility and, ultimately, victory for the Allies. Yet not one of the warring powers expected the war to end when it did. Certainly General Haig and his staff were planning offensive actions that would carry the war well into 1919. The beginning of 1918 saw the New Zealand Division recovering from its catastrophic defeat at Passchendaele the previous November. The New Zealanders were overjoyed to leave the Flanders region in early February. The fine spring weather of 1918 offered the chance to scrub off the mud and blood of the Third Battle of Ypres and the men's spirits and health began to revive.

It was to be the briefest of respites. Towards the end of March came news of a great disaster for the Allied cause. The German Army launched a massive offensive on 21 March, the *Kaiserschlacht* or the Kaiser's battle, aimed at winning the war before the armies of the United States joined their allies on the battlefield. The German offensive began well and broke the front of an entire British Army. The Fifth Army fell back nearly 40 miles to the Somme, with the Germans hard on their heels. The Germans then aimed to take the vital junction town of Amiens, a move that would cut the northern railway system and isolate the Channel ports. To help stem their advance, the New Zealand Division, along with other rested formations, was ordered to entrain for the Somme. These New Zealanders, having survived the horrors of Passchendaele, little imagined that they would soon be playing a crucial role in halting Germany's last attempt to win the war.

The New Zealanders were rushed to the Somme district to seal a 4-mile gap in the British line between Hébuterne and Beaumont-Hamel. The New Zealand Division not only plugged the gap in the nick of time, but then carried out a series of attacks to eject the Germans from the vital high ground to their front. It was an impressive feat of arms and one of New Zealand's most significant contributions to the Allied war effort.

The German spring offensive was eventually halted, the result of the stormtroops outrunning their artillery support and logistics chain, and then coming up against determined, fresh opposition. With the failure of this crucial attack in May 1918, there remained little potential for offensive action by the Germans for some time to come. It was the turn of the Allied armies to strike.

On 8 August 1918, the British armies in France launched the great offensive that became 'the Hundred Days' that ended the war in France. The Hundred Days was a significant military achievement, prompting the Allied Commander-in-Chief, Marshal

Ferdinand Foch, to remark, 'Never at any time in history has the British Army achieved greater results in attack than in this unbroken offensive.'

From 21 August, beginning with the battle of Bapaume, the New Zealand Division was in the thick of the action. Indeed, its involvement was almost continuous, and from August to November 1918 it was one of the spearhead divisions of the British Third Army. During this time it never experienced a reverse and came to be regarded as one of the best divisions in France. Morale was high during these months, as the New Zealand soldiers were convinced that they had the measure of their German opponents and that the Germans had lost heart. The reasons for the outstanding success of the New Zealand Division during this time were the calibre of its soldiers, its training, leadership and sheer size. The division also showed an aptitude for open warfare, the soldiers much preferring to be on the move rather than confined to the trenches, where they were at the mercy of the hostile climate, enemy artillery and snipers.

This last year of the war was certainly an eventful time for the New Zealand Division on the Western Front. It fought more actions here than in any other year of the war. While it was ultimately a successful year for the armies of Britain and its dominions (Canada, Australia, New Zealand, South Africa and Newfoundland), the success came at a very high price. In 1918, these armies experienced their greatest number of casualties. There were 830,000 casualties suffered between March and November 1918, with more than 300,000 casualties in the last three months of the war alone. The previous year, the Allies had suffered fewer casualties (818,000), despite losing every significant action in which they were engaged. In 1917, New Zealand forces had endured 6500 casualties at Messines and a further 7500 on the Passchendaele battlefields. In 1918, they experienced some 5000 casualties in March and April as they helped halt the German offensive, and a further 9000 during the Hundred Days.

Winning the war proved an expensive business for all concerned. It was particularly hard on those who, like the New Zealand Division, were at the front of the action.

In late March 1918, after three weeks of rest and training, the New Zealand Division was rushed to the Somme district to seal a huge gap in the line. New Zealand troops entrain for their new destination.
RICHARD MILDON H286

The rush to the Somme was the first time large numbers of New Zealand troops travelled by motorised transport. This continued for the rest of 1918. Here, New Zealand reinforcements are rushed into the front line near Grevillers on 2 September 1918.
NATIONAL ARMY MUSEUM 1993-1031 H991

New Zealand machine-gunners training at night near Rombly in northern France. A small mine has been detonated to their immediate front, making for a spectacular photograph. NATIONAL ARMY MUSEUM 1991-321 D3056

This image is rather mysterious. It has been previously published, with the caption noting these are New Zealanders in action on the Somme in 1916. Its original annotation states that it is: 'the 2nd Auckland Infantry Battalion in action at La Signy Farm, the Somme area, 30 March 1918. 16th Waikato Company with the 6th Hauraki on the right.' Subsequently, the publishers received a letter stating that the photograph in question was of New Zealand soldiers in action near Mailly-Maillet in 1918. The letter writer also claimed that the image was taken by a German soldier, who was bayoneted by the New Zealanders immediately after taking the photograph. The glass plate negative was then brought back to New Zealand.

It is impossible to know for sure where and when this image was taken or even how it was captured. However, it is, without doubt, one of the most graphic images of the war. NATIONAL ARMY MUSEUM 1990-106

A New Zealand soldier using a captured German machine gun near La Signy Farm on 6 April 1918.
NATIONAL ARMY MUSEUM
1993-1031 H484

Mealtime in the frontline trenches near La Signy Farm. The enemy trenches are less than 250 yards away.
NATIONAL ARMY MUSEUM
1999-111 H468

New Zealand stretcher-bearers bring in a wounded comrade while under shell-fire.
NATIONAL ARMY MUSEUM
1999-111 H485

The New Zealand Division joined the last great offensive of the war on 21 August 1918. Its first objective was the village of Puisieux, which it easily captured. In this image, the village is obscured by smoke and dust. NATIONAL ARMY MUSEUM 1990-1711

The ruins of Puisieux after the battle.
NATIONAL ARMY MUSEUM 1990-1711 H927

The New Zealanders captured over 100 German prisoners at Puisieux. Their own casualties were 17 men, who were all wounded. The prisoners in this photograph were captured at Puisieux and most look relieved to be out of the war. NATIONAL ARMY MUSEUM 1990-1711

Examining the papers of prisoners taken at Puisieux. The original annotation stated: 'The prisoner in the foreground, however, seems worried as to his fate, and wonders, perhaps, whether he will be eaten.'
NATIONAL ARMY MUSEUM
1997-21 H950

Tankdrome on the Western Front. These are the latest Mark V variety. The Allies had finally learned to integrate armour (that is, tanks) with infantry and artillery during an offensive. Most lead divisions in the great offensive had armoured support, although the New Zealand Division often found this to be a mixed blessing, as the tank crews fired on them on several occasions.
NATIONAL ARMY MUSEUM
2005-215

A Whippet scout tank in action near Grévillers. This one was in support of the New Zealand Division on 24 August 1918 and has just crossed a German trench. Whippet tanks were light and fast and offered excellent support to advancing infantry.
NATIONAL ARMY MUSEUM
1993-1031 H967

A New Zealand advanced dressing station treats soldiers wounded at Grévillers on 24 August 1918.

A German machine-gun position at Grévillers photographed just hours after its capture. By 1918 the German army defence relied almost solely on its numerous machine-gun positions. They caused the New Zealand Division serious problems in 1918 and inflicted most of the casualties. New Zealand soldiers hated them, but came to admire the courage of the German machine-gunners, most of whom died at their posts.

New Zealand machine-gunners occupy a captured German position near Puisieux on 21 August 1918. The boxes in the foreground contain German machine-gun ammunition. NATIONAL ARMY MUSEUM 1993-1031 H923

New Zealand soldiers take cover during a German artillery barrage near Achiet-le-Petit on 22 August 1918.

NATIONAL ARMY MUSEUM 1993-1031 H957

The devastation to the town of Bapaume shocked even the most battle-hardened New Zealanders. This image was taken from the Citadel on 4 September 1918. National Army Museum 1993-1031 H993

A British tank stranded near Bapaume. Even in 1918, tanks were still vulnerable to German artillery and impassable terrain. National Army Museum 1991-1951

One of the German soldiers responsible for the high level of casualties in 1918. The original annotation to this photograph reads, '"To the last" — a German machine-gunner. An unsung hero of the other side.'

Courage was admired by both sides in the war. Some machine-gunners, like the hero in this photograph, strapped themselves to their guns to prevent them from leaving their post. NATIONAL ARMY MUSEUM 1994-3346

German prisoners were often put to work bringing in wounded soldiers. These prisoners are carrying a wounded New Zealander near Puisieux on 21 August 1918.
NATIONAL ARMY MUSEUM 1993-1031 H976

New Zealand intelligence officers examine German prisoners.
NATIONAL ARMY MUSEUM
2005-215 H939

During the battle of Bapaume, New Zealand soldiers were attacked by German tanks for the first time in the war. German tanks, the A7V, were slow, unwieldy and needed a crew of 18 men. Only about 20 were produced. The New Zealand soldiers did not regard them as a great danger and the two that attacked here were soon knocked out of action. Curious New Zealand soldiers examine 'Schnuck'.
NATIONAL ARMY MUSEUM
1994-3346

A never-ending job on the Western Front. New Zealand Pioneers hard at work digging new trenches near Bapaume on 27 August 1918.
NATIONAL ARMY MUSEUM
1993-1031 H969

Guns captured by the New Zealand Division up to and including the battle of Bapaume.
NATIONAL ARMY MUSEUM 2005-749 H973

Constant digging was required. New Zealand engineers build strong defensive positions on the battlefield.
NATIONAL ARMY MUSEUM 1999-111 H487

A platoon of the New Zealand Rifle Brigade shelter behind a bank and fill their water bottles before going into action on 22 August 1918 near Achiet-le-Petit.
NATIONAL ARMY MUSEUM 1993-1031 H959

A New Zealand band entertains some of the residents of Le Quesnoy on a wet afternoon.
NATIONAL ARMY MUSEUM
2005-749

In August–September 1918, the Allies were pressing the Germans against the Hindenburg Line and in mid-September they breached this formidable obstacle in several places. This image shows part of the barbed wire entanglement that marked the beginning of the Hindenburg Line.
NATIONAL ARMY MUSEUM 1991-321 D1340

A successful raiding party from the New Zealand Rifle Brigade displays the 13 machine guns they have captured in the raid.
NATIONAL ARMY MUSEUM
1997-21 H832

The Maori Pioneers welcome Prime Minister William Massey and his coalition partner Sir Joseph Ward with a stirring haka. This photograph was taken at the end of June 1918.
NATIONAL ARMY MUSEUM
1993-1031 H680

Brigadier Napier Johnston explains the significance of the terrain to Massey and Ward on 1 July 1918.
NATIONAL ARMY MUSEUM
1993-1031 H676

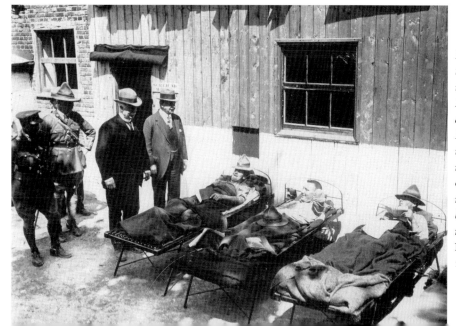

Massey and Ward visit the sick and lightly wounded in the New Zealand field ambulance at Authie on 1 July 1918. Massey also insisted on visiting the seriously wounded when he could, occasions that often reduced him to tears but earned the grudging respect of the soldiers.
NATIONAL ARMY MUSEUM
1993-1031 H716

General Russell snatches some rest. He was not a well man in 1918 and this did affect his performance, particularly during the battle of Bapaume.
NATIONAL ARMY MUSEUM 1990-1711 H780

Some officers of the Wellington Regiment. From left to right they are: Captains J.N. Rauch, R.L. Evatt, J. Macmorran, Lieutenant R. Witherford, Captain L.T. Herbert and Lieutenant C.G. Robinson. In 1918 these men were experienced junior officers; their decisions meant life or death for the men they commanded and often for themselves too. NATIONAL ARMY MUSEUM 1990-1711

Anzac Corps Commander and later an Army commander, General William Birdwood chats with New Zealand officers. Birdwood had distinguished himself at Gallipoli and was a favourite with both Australian and New Zealand soldiers. NATIONAL ARMY MUSEUM 2004-193 H791

New Zealand soldiers cheer the Prince of Wales (later Edward VII), who is saluting them. The Prince is escorted by Brigadier C.W. Melvill and Colonel W.H. Cunningham. NATIONAL ARMY MUSEUM 1990-1711 H1063

The battle-scarred village of Foncquevillers just behind the front line. NATIONAL ARMY MUSEUM 1997-21 H869

As the Germans retreated in France they left a trail of destruction behind. As the original annotation stated, this was a typical scene of a factory in Beauvois that had been 'wantonly destroyed by the enemy'. NATIONAL ARMY MUSEUM 1997-21 H1092

(sandstorms) and a monotonous diet of bully beef and biscuits. Despite these discomforts, conditions here were better than on the Western Front.

The progress of the campaign hinged on logistical supply, especially the availability of water for troops and horses. During the campaign New Zealand horses developed a reputation for being able to go for long periods without water — between 60 and 70 hours when really tested. The horses suffered the same privations as their masters during this war, but also had to put up with 'flu', ringworm, sand colic and sores around the mouth and eyes caused by the ever-present flies. In all, New Zealand sent nearly 10,000 horses to this campaign; only one is known to have returned. At the end of the campaign most of the New Zealand horses were kept for the Occupation Force, but some of the older horses were shot, one of the hardest tasks New Zealand soldiers have ever had to perform. To make things easier, squadrons exchanged those horses condemned to death by their age or condition, so that no soldier had to shoot a horse from his own squadron. The dead horses, many with more battle scars than their owners, were left in rows along the Mediterranean shore.

The first action of the New Zealand Mounteds was in the vicinity of Romani, some 18 miles east of the Suez Canal. Sent there in April 1916 to patrol the desert, dig wells and report on Turkish movements, the New Zealanders proved adept at this style of warfare. The Turks responded to the build-up of troops and supplies at Romani, attacking it with 14,000 troops on 4 August 1916. The attack was anticipated and the British positions were well prepared. It was repulsed, with heavy losses for the Turks. About 5000 Turks were killed or wounded in this battle, and a further 4000 captured over the five days of fighting. As the Turks withdrew back across the desert, the Anzac Mounted Division pursued them.

The battle of Romani established a pattern that was to persist for much of the campaign. This pattern was one of coping with the trying conditions of the Sinai Desert and Palestine, active patrolling to gather information and harass the enemy, and flashpoints of action.

Once an adequate water supply was established at Romani, which did not happen until November 1916, the British forces felt themselves able to advance across the Sinai Desert. El Arish was taken on 21 December and Magdhaba two days later. Rafa, on the Egypt-Palestine border, was attacked in January 1917, with the New Zealand Mounted Rifles Brigade carrying out a successful flanking manoeuvre that brought the brigade in on the enemy's rear. Rafa was taken, along with 1500 Turkish prisoners.

With the completion of a water pipeline and railhead to Rafa, the Allied conquest of Palestine began. Gaza was the Allies' first objective and it was nearly taken in March after the Anzac Mounted Division completed a successful envelopment of the town. But with success in their grasp and the Turks preparing to evacuate, the British commander ordered a halt to the attack on Gaza and withdrew the force back to Rafa. It was a bitter disappointment for the Anzac Mounted troops.

The second attack on Gaza occurred in mid-April 1917, but the Turks, under the able leadership of the German commander, Colonel Friedrich von Kressenstein, had strengthened the Gaza defences and were expecting the attack. It was a costly failure for the Allies, even though they were able to use tanks and gas in this theatre of war for the first time. Their losses numbered 6500, and this disaster led to a series of command changes. The British commander, Lieutenant General Sir Archibald Murray, was replaced by General Sir Edmund Allenby. Harry Chauvel was elevated to command what eventually became the Desert Mounted Corps, so becoming the first Australian officer to lead an army corps. Edward Chaytor was promoted to major general and took over the Anzac Mounted Division, the only New Zealander to command an Anzac force at this level.

Allenby was determined to break into Palestine and set about doing this by focusing on Beersheba, which was encircled by the Anzac Mounteds and captured in a famous charge by the 4th Australian Light Horse. Fighting continued for another week before the Turkish frontier defences broke and the Turks withdrew.

After a dash across the coastal plains, the New Zealand Mounted Rifles Brigade captured Ayun Kara near Richon le Zion, on 14 November. It then held the small village against fierce Turkish counterattacks, which cost the New Zealanders 174 casualties, one of the heaviest tolls of the campaign. Many of those involved in the action at Ayun Kara regarded it, as one trooper later recorded, as 'easily the fiercest fighting we have seen'. Two days later, the New Zealanders galloped into Jaffa. Jerusalem was taken on 11 December, as 'a Christmas present to the British nation', to use the words of the British Prime Minister, Lloyd George. It was a great morale boost in the hardest year of the war.

Jericho was the next objective set and it was taken on 21 February 1918, after a successful outflanking manoeuvre by the New Zealand Mounted Rifles Brigade.

After occupying the unhealthy Jordan Valley through the discomforts of summer, the Anzac Mounteds took part in General Allenby's final offensive against the Turks and Germans in September 1918. The decisive attack was directed against Megiddo, while the Anzac Mounteds and attached troops carried out an important diversionary action. Crossing the Jordan River on 22 September, they captured Amman and Es Salt, which had beaten off two earlier attempts to take them. More than 10,000 prisoners were taken at Amman.

The Turkish Army was now in full retreat and the Anzac Mounteds pursued them relentlessly, covering some 45 miles in five days. They were the first of Allenby's troops to enter Damascus on 1 October and pushed on northwards to Aleppo. With her army disintegrating, and her Central Power allies nearing collapse under the weight of continuing Allied offensives and blockades, Turkey requested an armistice, which came into effect on 31 October 1918.

Unfortunately, after the armistice the impressive record of the New Zealand troopers was marred by several incidents of indiscipline and brutality towards the local inhabitants. The worst of these occurred when, in retaliation for the death of a New Zealand trooper during a robbery, New Zealanders and some Australians massacred about 40 of the male population of the village of Surafend, and then burned the village and a nearby Bedouin camp. The Surafend massacre is the worst atrocity known to have been committed by New Zealand troops serving on operations. Despite several courts of inquiry, no one was ever tried or punished for this war crime. The village of Surafend was later rebuilt by the British Army, which then billed the Australian and New Zealand governments for the cost.

Panorama of Zeitoun Camp, Egypt. Zeitoun was the location for the New Zealand Headquarters in Sinai-Palestine. NATIONAL ARMY MUSEUM 2006-88

A home among the cacti. Sergeant Jim Comer of the New Zealand Mounted Field Ambulance admitted that he looked 'pretty rough' and 'very skinny' in this photograph. He also pointed out it was extremely hot when the snap was taken.
NATIONAL ARMY MUSEUM 1994-2960

Troopers of the Wellington Mounted Rifles playing poker in the limited shade offered by this makeshift shelter. Note that their rifles, with fixed bayonets, have been used as tent poles.
NATIONAL ARMY MUSEUM 2005-88

Troopers of the Auckland Mounted Rifles take a snack break while on patrol. The original annotation stated that 'the heat is so intense that it is impossible to remain without a shade'.
NATIONAL ARMY MUSEUM 1996-946

Camouflaged tents in the inhospitable Jordan Valley.
NATIONAL ARMY MUSEUM 1993-2761

Contrary to some beliefs, the New Zealand Mounted Rifles Brigade did not have an easy war. To the heat, sand and flies could be added the necessity of constructing defences, including trenches. Here, some troopers practise constructing personal shelters.
NATIONAL ARMY MUSEUM 2005-500

Trenches being constructed to defend the Suez Canal in early 1916. NATIONAL ARMY MUSEUM 1992-757

Constructing defences near Gaza.
MATTHEW POMEROY

Model trenches constructed as part of the Suez Canal defences in 1916. NATIONAL ARMY MUSEUM 1992-757

New Zealand troopers building a road for the artillery over a wadi near Gaza. The soldier on the left with a pick is Trooper Ross Lange of Hawera.
NATIONAL ARMY MUSEUM 1996-946

As the Egyptian Expeditionary Force pushed the Turks eastward into Palestine, the railway quickly followed the advancing army. It had to in order to provide the logistics necessary to sustain military operations. A water pipeline was also constructed. This photograph shows the railway being extended from the Suez Canal eastward.
NATIONAL ARMY MUSEUM 1996-946

In good conditions engineers and their Egyptian labourers could build more than a mile of track a day.
NATIONAL ARMY MUSEUM 1993-1213

Troopers of the Auckland Mounted Rifles going up the line.
NATIONAL ARMY MUSEUM 1992-1153

197

Bedouin Arabs patiently wait their turn for access to a water supply. NATIONAL ARMY MUSEUM 1993-1213

These Egyptians were employed to handle the camels of the 15th Company, Imperial Camel Corps. NATIONAL ARMY MUSEUM 1988-1482

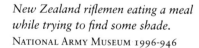
New Zealand riflemen eating a meal while trying to find some shade. NATIONAL ARMY MUSEUM 1996-946

New Zealand troopers of the 15th Company, Imperial Camel Corps, receive Christmas parcels from the people of Wellington. This photograph was taken near Rafa at the end of 1916. NATIONAL ARMY MUSEUM 1988-1482

The horse and its handler's skill were vital in the Sinai-Palestine theatre of war. So successful were the Anzac Mounteds and Light Horse in this campaign that, instead of the subsidiary role for which they were meant, they became the main strike force of the Egyptian Expeditionary Force. A New Zealand Mounted Rifles trooper ready for action.
NATIONAL ARMY MUSEUM
1992-1153

The bond between horse and rider was exceptionally strong. 'Me and Bill': 'Me' is Trooper Stanley Langdale, Auckland Mounted Rifles.
NATIONAL ARMY MUSEUM
1992-754

A New Zealand Mounted Rifles trooper ready for a long patrol.
NATIONAL ARMY MUSEUM
1994-3467

Troops of the Auckland Mounted Rifles pose with their horses, which look in the peak of condition.
National Army Museum 1992-1153, National Army Museum 1994-3467

A packhorse carries a Hotchkiss machine gun and ammunition.
National Army Museum
1996-946

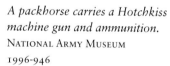

The annotation 'A faithful friend' reveals the importance of the horse in this campaign. The frilly strings on the bridle are designed to keep the flies away from the horse's eyes.
National Army Museum
1992-1153

Farrier Sergeant Westwood and horse rest during one of the Gaza battles. Lyn Murphy

Horses ready for inspection.
National Army Museum 1992-754

Horse fodder in the Army Service Corps yard ready for distribution. Fodder and forage were readily available for the horses. Water was more difficult to find.
National Army Museum 2000-876

How some of the fodder reached the horses.
National Army Museum 1994-3467

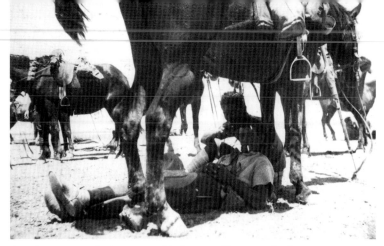

Horses often became sick and also became casualties. When that occurred, replacements (known as remounts) were needed. Breaking in a horse at the remount depot. NATIONAL ARMY MUSEUM 1993-1213

As a last resort, the horses could also provide some shade. Trooper L. Dulovan of the Wellington Mounted Rifles seeks shelter under his horse. NATIONAL ARMY MUSEUM 2005-882

Swimming horses in the Suez Canal in March 1915. NATIONAL ARMY MUSEUM 2000-876

Arabs, in the secret pay of the Egyptian Expeditionary Force, at Amman near the Hejaz railway. NATIONAL ARMY MUSEUM 2005-882

Horses were casualties, too. Horses killed by bombs at Romani on 1 June 1916. National Army Museum 1996-946

The fate of some of the Auckland Mounted Rifles' horses killed in this same bombing raid. National Army Museum 1986-1136

These horses were killed when the Auckland Mounted Rifles' headquarters in the Jordan Valley were bombed. National Army Museum 1996-946

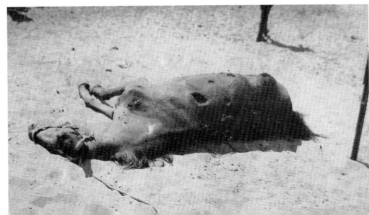

The shrapnel wounds on this victim of a bomb blast are clearly visible. National Army Museum 1993-1294

B Squadron of the Wellington Mounted Rifles takes a welcome break. NATIONAL ARMY MUSEUM 2000-876

Two 15th Company troopers seem at home on their mounts.
NATIONAL ARMY MUSEUM 1988-1482

While they did not play as vital a role as horses, camels were also used extensively by the Egyptian Expeditionary Force. Camels being trucked to the front.
NATIONAL ARMY MUSEUM 1988-1482

Camels were much more difficult to handle than horses. The 15th Company, Imperial Camel Corps were all New Zealand troopers. NATIONAL ARMY MUSEUM 1992-745

The 15th Company, Imperial Camel Corps on the march near Wadi El Arish on 23 December 1916.
NATIONAL ARMY MUSEUM 1996-946

Camels were also used to carry food, water and other supplies. NATIONAL ARMY MUSEUM 1993-2761

Camels carry fodder at Zeitoun Camp.
NATIONAL ARMY MUSEUM 1990-1712

Camels were also used to carry wounded men. Here, a camel ambulance is being loaded with wounded Turkish soldiers on 23 December 1916. National Army Museum 1996-946

Some wounded troopers carried by camel. This photograph was taken by an Australian Light Horseman. The wounded are riding in chairs strapped on both sides of the camel. While the men look cheerful, the camel's slow, awkward gait and the long distances travelled made for a painful journey. National Army Museum 1996-946

New Zealand troopers bathe with their camels in the Mediterranean. National Army Museum 1988-1482

Camels also became casualties during the campaign. These camels were killed when a German plane dropped four bombs on the camp. Forty-one camels and three horses were killed. Twenty-one troopers also became casualties.
NATIONAL ARMY MUSEUM
1988-1482

In another bombing raid at Abu Sitta, 13 camels were killed.
NATIONAL ARMY MUSEUM
1993-1220

A difficult task. A trooper prepares to shoot a badly wounded camel.
NATIONAL ARMY MUSEUM
1993-1220

*Constructing a water
supply in the desert.
Water was the key to the
success of using horse-
mounted infantry in this
theatre of war. Finding
good supplies of water
for horses and soldiers
was a priority task.*
NATIONAL ARMY MUSEUM
1990-1712

*Watering horses using a
channel dug in the sand.*
ROSEMARY HICKS

Using a petrol pump to draw water from an ancient well. NATIONAL ARMY MUSEUM 1996-946

Horses watering at the Wadi Hesi on the eve of the Ayun Kara battle. NATIONAL ARMY MUSEUM 1986-2089

Watering horses during operations.
NATIONAL ARMY MUSEUM 1996-946

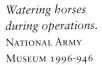

Watering horses in the Jordan River.
NATIONAL ARMY MUSEUM 1996-946

Annotated 'A welcome sup', this photograph shows a trooper and Egyptian handler of the Wellington Mounted Rifles watering horses at a desert oasis.
NATIONAL ARMY MUSEUM
2000-876

Horse fodder waiting at Port Said for loading and shipment to Bir-el-Bela.
NATIONAL ARMY MUSEUM
1996-946

A rest at the end of a hard day and time for a hot meal.
NATIONAL ARMY MUSEUM
2005-882

A New Zealand Mounted Rifles regiment moves out ready for action. LYN MURPHY

The New Zealand Mounted Rifles units labelled this place Diahorea [sic] Valley. Its real name was slightly more attractive: Tel el Nag. MATTHEW POMEROY

Annotated 'Duds', this photograph shows a New Zealand trooper posing behind some unexploded shells. The largest shell is likely to have been fired by a naval gun. NATIONAL ARMY MUSEUM 1993-1220

Identification and burial of the Anzac dead after the battle of Romani. NATIONAL ARMY MUSEUM 1993-1299

An unexploded Turkish mine. These did cause casualties and had to be handled with care — something the Anzac troops often overlooked to their cost.
NATIONAL ARMY MUSEUM 1993-1299

Heads down. A Turkish landmine in action.
NATIONAL ARMY MUSEUM
1993-1220

The aftermath of a Turkish mine not given due respect.
NATIONAL ARMY MUSEUM
1992-1299

An armoured train, with machine guns for protection.
NATIONAL ARMY MUSEUM 1994-3467

Lieutenant Sommerville and Trooper J.F. Smith of B Squadron, Wellington Mounted Rifles, observe from a sand ridge in the desert. NATIONAL ARMY MUSEUM 2000-876

Troopers run during a series of explosions at Zeitoun Camp. NATIONAL ARMY MUSEUM 1993-1213

Troopers of 9th Squadron, Wellington Mounted Rifles, shooting on a range constructed in the desert.
National Army Museum 2005-882

Trooper A. Thomas practising on the Hotchkiss gun. The Hotchkiss replaced the heavier Lewis gun in mid-1916. David Mowat

Albert Creed of the Canterbury Mounted Rifles in a sniper's position in the desert. Albert, a Gallipoli veteran, posted this photograph to his family for Christmas 1917. David Mowat

A Vickers machine-gun team in the anti-aircraft role. The troopers in the photograph are B. Bird, H. Farmer and D. McKendrick.
National Army Museum 1992-754

A New Zealand machine-gun team in action against the Turks. NATIONAL ARMY MUSEUM 2007-518

British soldiers awaiting burial after the debacle of the first Gaza battle. NATIONAL ARMY MUSEUM 1993-1220

One of the 'landships' brought to Palestine for the big push on Gaza. This one was named Kia Ora by an Auckland Mounted Rifles trooper. The tank has a covering with branches thrown over it to avoid detection from the air. This photograph was taken at Belah in May 1917. NATIONAL ARMY MUSEUM 1996-946

In the trenches. A New Zealand Mounted Rifles trooper prepares to fire his rifle in action.
National Army Museum 2005-882

No way to treat a lady, however deadly. The famous gun 'Jericho Jane' abandoned by the retreating Turks and left upside down in a wadi.

Source unknown

National Army Museum 1996-946

The clean-up after the action at Rafa on 24 December 1916. This is a burial party of the Auckland Mounted Rifles and there are six to eight dead soldiers in this stretch of trench. Trooper Dave Nesbitt is the soldier using the spade in the foreground. NATIONAL ARMY MUSEUM 1996-946

The burial of Private Fred Crum, Mounted Field Ambulance, at Belah on 9 May 1917. MATTHEW POMEROY

Dead Turkish soldiers dumped in a disused well.
<small>NATIONAL ARMY MUSEUM</small>
1993-1299

The remains of Turkish soldiers who were bayoneted while trying to escape.
<small>NATIONAL ARMY MUSEUM</small>
1993-1220

Turkish wounded being loaded on to ambulances after the action at Magdhaba. They faced a rough journey of 28 miles before being transferred to trains for a 200-mile journey to Cairo.
<small>NATIONAL ARMY MUSEUM</small>
1996-946

Loading wounded men on to ambulances after a recent action.
National Army Museum
1996-946

A wounded trooper is carried to treatment. He looks to be enjoying the experience. The man on the right carrying the stretcher is the trooper's corporal, R.M. Stevens, who was at this hospital for suspected diphtheria. It probably explains the trooper's smile. National Army Museum 1996-946

A couple of wounded mates of the Auckland Mounted Rifles.
National Army Museum
1996-946

A field ambulance on the way to Cairo. National Army Museum 1993-1213

The 17th British General Hospital at Alexandria. The seriously wounded often spent time here.
NATIONAL ARMY MUSEUM 1988-1753

Turkish soldiers bury their dead before being taken into captivity.
NATIONAL ARMY MUSEUM 1996-946

Troopers perform a burial service at a lonely grave in the desert.
NATIONAL ARMY MUSEUM 1993-1213

The graves of Corporal J.W. Sutherland, Auckland Mounted Rifles, and Corporal Woods, New Zealand Machine Gun Brigade, both killed at Amman on 30 March 1918.
NATIONAL ARMY MUSEUM 1996-946

Graves of Auckland Mounted Rifles troopers at Richon le Zion. NATIONAL ARMY MUSEUM 1992-1153

Troopers capture some stray Turks on a patrol. NATIONAL ARMY MUSEUM 1993-1213

At rest in the shade. The grave of a trooper in the Canterbury Mounted Rifles. NATIONAL ARMY MUSEUM 1992-1153

A large portion of the work done by the New Zealand Mounted Rifles Brigade involved long, arduous patrols. Sometimes these were fighting patrols and raids, but more often than not they were for reconnaissance. Troopers of the Wellington Mounted Rifles on a reconnaissance patrol in Palestine. NATIONAL ARMY MUSEUM 2005-882

This patrol has come across an Egyptian working party making a cutting for the railway.
NATIONAL ARMY MUSEUM
1996-946

A troop from the Auckland Mounted Rifles cross the Jordan River.
NATIONAL ARMY MUSEUM
1996-946

New Zealand troopers in the Judean Hills.
NATIONAL ARMY MUSEUM
1996-946

Troopers cross a newly constructed bridge built by the New Zealand engineers.
NATIONAL ARMY MUSEUM
1992-757

233

Troopers of the Auckland Mounted Rifles in a cornfield. From left to right they are: Troopers Martin, Donaldson, Storey, Heath, Macey, Sutherland, Thornton, Maddox, Welsh and Chandler. NATIONAL ARMY MUSEUM 1996-946

Auckland Mounted Rifles horsemen on the road to Bethlehem. NATIONAL ARMY MUSEUM 1996-946

Part of the New Zealand Mounted Rifles Brigade return to camp to water their horses after an action at Bir-el-Abd in 1916.
NATIONAL ARMY MUSEUM
1993-1294

New Zealand Mounted Rifles troopers at Es Salt, scene of severe fighting on two occasions.
NATIONAL ARMY MUSEUM 1992-1153

German prisoners being escorted by New Zealand Mounted Rifles troops march past the walls of Jerusalem. The prisoners were captured on 14 July 1918. NATIONAL ARMY MUSEUM 1986-2089

Not dead, just absolutely exhausted. A trooper and horse resting after a 'stunt'.
NATIONAL ARMY MUSEUM
1993-1299

Boys firing at Taube Sainai

Turkish Taube Sainai

New Zealand Mounted Rifles troopers fire at a Turkish Taube aircraft in the Sinai.
NATIONAL ARMY MUSEUM 1993-1294

It does not look as if they hit it.
NATIONAL ARMY MUSEUM 1993-1294

Flying these fragile planes in this region was hazardous, as the next four images reveal. The remains of a crashed British plane at Matruh.
NATIONAL ARMY MUSEUM 1990-409

Also at Matruh and also beyond repair.
NATIONAL ARMY MUSEUM 1990-409

Annotated 'A nice little smash', this photograph shows a British plane that has landed nose first at Kharu in Palestine. NATIONAL ARMY MUSEUM 1996-946

Not much remains of this German Albatross plane brought down at Abu-Sitta. NATIONAL ARMY MUSEUM 1993-1220

This German plane fared better. It was brought down in one piece. NATIONAL ARMY MUSEUM 1993-1294

A British plane operating near Gaza draws plenty of observers. NATIONAL ARMY MUSEUM 1996-946

Real horsepower. A British plane being pulled by a team of horses. NATIONAL ARMY MUSEUM 2005-882

New Zealand troopers view some dead Turks killed in action at Darmiah. NATIONAL ARMY MUSEUM 1986-2089

Turkish dead removed from the Damu Bridge. The Turks were in full retreat when this photograph was taken on 22 September 1918. NATIONAL ARMY MUSEUM 1996-946

Service in the Middle East offered New Zealand troops the opportunity to visit places they knew only through attendance at Sunday School and church, including such attractions as the Jaffa gates of the Holy City. NATIONAL ARMY MUSEUM 1991-2409

The view through a mule's ears. A New Zealand Mounted Rifles trooper on the road to Luxor.
HERBERT RIX

A party of Auckland Mounted Rifles troopers out sightseeing.
NATIONAL ARMY MUSEUM
1996-946

If time and circumstances permitted, a visit to the pyramids and Sphinx were a 'must do'.
NATIONAL ARMY MUSEUM
1996-946

Two thirsty troopers take a break from sightseeing.
NATIONAL ARMY MUSEUM 1992-1153

Fishing in the Jordan River provided some entertainment. Using Mills bombs, though, as this trooper has done, tended to take the sport out of it. NATIONAL ARMY MUSEUM 1992-754

The troopers were excellent at making their own entertainment in quiet times. A game of draughts among the cacti. Sergeant Jim Comer of the New Zealand Field Artillery is the soldier on the left.
NATIONAL ARMY MUSEUM 1994-2960

Sergeant Comer on the right this time enjoys a game of crib. As he wrote on the back: 'Anything to pass away a few dull minutes'. Comer also wrote, 'Of course, I'm not in my Sunday clothes'.
NATIONAL ARMY MUSEUM 1994-2960

Pancakes and camp life for the Canterbury Mounted Rifles troopers. HERBERT RIX

Members of Otago Mounted Rifles enjoy a dip at Ismailia. This photograph was probably taken in 1915, as they sailed for France with the New Zealand Division early in 1916. PAULINE WILKINSON

Brigade races at Rafa. This event occurred after the Armistice. NATIONAL ARMY MUSEUM 2005-882

Troopers of the Wellington Mounted Rifles enjoy an illicit game of two-up at Zeitoun Camp.
NATIONAL ARMY MUSEUM
2000-876

A tug-of-war competition attracts an audience.
NATIONAL ARMY MUSEUM
2005-882

Troopers of the Wellington Mounted Rifles playing donkey polo.
NATIONAL ARMY MUSEUM 2000-876, NATIONAL ARMY MUSEUM 2000-876

Troopers and horses enjoy a romp in the Mediterranean surf.
NATIONAL ARMY MUSEUM 1993-1213, NATIONAL ARMY MUSEUM 2005-882

Troopers of the Wellington Mounted Rifles wrestle on horseback.
NATIONAL ARMY MUSEUM 2005-882, NATIONAL ARMY MUSEUM 1993-1213

The fate of many of the New Zealand Mounted Rifles Brigade's oldest horses, and those in poor condition, after the war. Some had as many battle scars as their riders. HERBERT RIX

A four-man section ready for action. The New Zealand Mounted Rifles Brigade was an outstanding military formation that did all that was asked of it. The quality of its troopers was superb. HERBERT RIX

Return to Gallipoli. Canterbury Mounted Rifles troopers pose at the guns of the Turkish fort of Kilid Bahr. NATIONAL ARMY MUSEUM 1992-1153

249

One can only guess at the sound this handmade, one-string violin produced. NATIONAL ARMY MUSEUM 1988-1482

Some troopers farewell a mate who is soon to return to New Zealand. HERBERT RIX

All New Zealanders and keen to get home. HERBERT RIX

Life on the Western Front 1916–18

The New Zealand Division spent nearly three years in France and Belgium. After the Armistice it then spent a number of months as part of an occupying force in Germany. This was a considerable length of time for impressionable young men and the experience was one they never forgot. It should be noted that the three years on the Western Front were not all spent in offensive action, nor was the Division in the front line for most of that time.

Offensive campaigns such as those at the Somme in 1916 or at Passchendaele the following year were actually unusual occurrences. They were 'the exception rather than the rule', according to Professor Richard Holmes. One of the reasons for this is that such campaigns required a long, measured build-up of men and resources. The climate and terrain also mitigated against constant fighting. However, when major offensives did occur, they were deadly to those taking part. One officer who served on the Western Front likened these offensive battles to a powerful, destructive storm. Colonel Walter Nicholson recorded of them: 'Trench fighting goes on throughout the war, but a battle comes like a hailstorm, mows down a field of corn, and is over for a year.'

If these destructive, lethal storms were rare occurrences, service in the frontline trenches was all too common. By the time the New Zealand Division arrived in France, a cyclical pattern for garrisoning the trenches was well established and the New Zealanders soon became part of it. The cycle comprised four steps: time spent in the frontline trenches, time in the reserve positions, time at rest and time moving from one location to another. Even when a division was at the very sharp end of this cycle — the frontline trench, which could sometimes be only a few hundred metres away from the German positions — not all its members were present. Usually, only two brigades were sent forward and one was held in reserve. Furthermore, the two forward brigades usually only had half their strength — that is, two battalions — in line and these would be frequently rotated through the forward trenches. Brigades also followed a rotation policy decided by divisional headquarters.

When a division was in the trenches, there was little opportunity for rest. Those units not in the front line were busy with the myriad tasks necessary to maintain a fighting position. The men were constantly digging to improve the trenches or repair damage. Wiring parties were always in demand. Rations and supplies had to be carried to the frontline trenches — a thankless, demanding and dangerous task. Danger lurked everywhere; German artillery, mortar fire or snipers could strike at any time. Equally unpredictable, but nonetheless deadly, were careless friends and allies. Life in the front line was a hard, uncomfortable and dangerous existence.

What made this experience tolerable was the presence of close friends, and NCOs and officers who shared the danger and provided leadership when it was most needed. Religiously following a known routine also helped. Little comforts such as regular mail, good food, hot tea, cigarettes and the rum ration assumed an importance and restorative quality out of all proportion to their reality. In their world of chance, danger and discomfort, the little things really mattered to the men at the front.

They mattered away from the front, too, where a hot bath, clean clothes, hot and plentiful food and rest meant so much to soldiers who had endured the trials of earth and wire at the front. So did interaction with the local populace. Away from the front, the divisions of the British Expeditionary Force were billeted in French or Belgian towns, villages and farmhouses. Here, they had the opportunity to mix with local civilians. They also had the chance to purchase local food and wine at the shops and bars that sprung up wherever soldiers were billeted. No doubt other wares were also for sale too.

The relationship between New Zealand soldiers and the French civilians they encountered is captured in this brief passage from Ormond Burton's book *The Silent Division*. Burton was an infantry soldier in the 2nd Auckland Battalion and he records a telling scene when the New Zealanders learn in March 1918 that they must leave their pleasant village to help stem the German advance on the Somme. Burton wrote:

As the men marched to the railway siding the village people came out into the streets to bid good-bye to the guests who in so short a while had become their friends. Rough jests flew round.

'*Bonsoir*, mademoiselle, you promenade with me?'

'After de *prochaine* war, per-r-r-raps!'

'Hullo, Marie! How's the beer standing?'

'*Allons, gourmand!* You have drunk all de *biere* — no more left for nex *soldat*!'

'*Au revoir*, madame! *Encore* six *oeufs* when we come back — and *beaucoup* chips!

'Ah, Madeleine! You *embrassez-moi* for *bonne chance*!'

'*Allons! Brigand!* You kiss too many *mademoiselles* — me write your *fiancée*, tell her you no good!'

'*Au revoir, petite! Au revoir, madame!*'

'Ha, Berthe! Me see promenade with *officier* last night!'

'*Allons! Scelerat!* You *beaucoup* zigzag las' night — too much *vin blanc.*'

But under all the merry badinage ran a deeper tone, for after all this was a supreme hour in the agony of France. Who knew what might befall if these men failed to stay the onward rush to Amiens? In a few days other battalions might march along these roads — battalions of men in grey-green uniforms, the enemies of France. The men who marched away were not Frenchmen, but they were the friends of France, and in a few hours they would step into the breach and hold for France.

'*Dieu vous aide, messieurs! Dieu vous garde! Vous combattez pour nous! St Jeanne d'Arc vous aide! Nous prions pour vous!*'

And so amid laughter and prayers the men marched away to the Second Battle of the Somme.

This interaction with the locals was important for the New Zealanders and it made a lasting impression on them. This is certainly evident in their letters, diaries and photographs of the time and in their recollections years after the war.

This section of photographs looks at life in France and Belgium away from the trenches and the deadly offensives. It tries to capture something of the complexity of that experience which, for many New Zealand soldiers, was part of the rich fabric of their war on the Western Front. It was something these New Zealanders remembered for the rest of their lives.

An officers' dugout in the close support line near Chards Farm on the Somme. National Army Museum 2007-183

These New Zealand soldiers seem at home in their 'Kiwi Dugout' in Belgium. Mark Febery

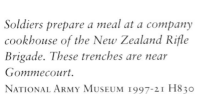

Soldiers prepare a meal at a company cookhouse of the New Zealand Rifle Brigade. These trenches are near Gommecourt.
National Army Museum 1997-21 H830

New Zealanders in the support line waiting to go into the frontline trenches. While some men sleep in the 'funk holes', one soldier uses the opportunity to write a letter home and another cleans his rifle.
National Army Museum 1993-1031 H508

A party of engineers rest and take shelter in a massive shell hole near Spree Farm. NATIONAL ARMY MUSEUM 1997-21

A New Zealand soldier takes the opportunity to purchase some local produce.
NATIONAL ARMY MUSEUM 1992-773 H32

Another New Zealand soldier helps a local woman relocate to a safer place.
NATIONAL ARMY MUSEUM 1999-111 H506

The sad plight of many French civilians touched the hearts of New Zealand soldiers and hardened their resolve to see the war eventually won. Here, a group of locals search through what used to be their homes.
NATIONAL ARMY MUSEUM 1991-584

Buying sweets from a young local. NATIONAL ARMY MUSEUM 1992-773 H655

Preparing for pay day. NCOs check the million francs that will be paid to soldiers of the New Zealand Division. This event occurred twice a month.
National Army Museum 1993-1031 H421

A very welcome moment. New Zealand soldiers being paid prior to heading for leave in the United Kingdom.
National Army Museum 1993-1032 H102

A crowded church service and a time to remember. This was a special service: the All Souls Day Memorial Service on 2 November 1917.
National Army Museum 1999-111 H368

An open air church parade held at Louvencourt on 30 April 1918.

National Army Museum 1993-1031 H554

Sergeant Robert Arthur Bruere loads 18-pounder ammunition into an artillery limber. His footwear is very unusual. Neil Bruere

New Zealand engineers testing the water quality.
National Army Museum 1987-1363 H591

New Zealand machine-gunners fitting rounds into the machine-gun belts.
National Army Museum 1999-111 H583

A soldier from the Canterbury Regiment shoeing mules.
<small>NATIONAL ARMY MUSEUM</small>
1999-111 H318

Soldiers in the New Zealand Veterinary Corps check on a horse at Louvencourt on 22 August 1918.
<small>NATIONAL ARMY MUSEUM</small>
1993-1031 H600

A soldier looks for lice in his clothing. All soldiers on the Western Front were lice-infested — it came with the job. Whenever possible, soldiers conducted lice hunts like this. It gave only temporary relief, though.
<small>NATIONAL ARMY MUSEUM</small> 1992-773 H36

Soldiers await their turn at the Divisional Baths at Bertrancourt. A bath after a stint in the trenches was an eagerly anticipated and welcome luxury. National Army Museum 1999-111 H545

Keeping the hair cropped short helped in the control of lice. A haircut on the Somme for artillery officers. They are Major Rodger, Captain Ellis and Lieutenant Downey. National Army Museum 1990-1712

Fumigation measures and disinfecting blankets and underclothes also helped to control lice. They were never eradicated, though.

National Army Museum 1993-1032 H248

National Army Museum 1993-1031 H505

Clean and refreshed, soldiers dress after their bath.
NATIONAL ARMY MUSEUM
1993-1032 H104

'Sock duty'. A group of soldiers busy washing socks. The original annotation stated that 4000 pairs of socks were washed daily by a team of 20 men, the youngest of whom was 45 years old.
NATIONAL ARMY MUSEUM
1993-1031 H563

Sacks of loaves of bread leave the First New Zealand Field Bakery at Rouen on 5 July 1918.
NATIONAL ARMY MUSEUM
1993-1031 H771

The Cook's Fatigue Party. These soldiers seem happy enough to assist the cook (in the white apron) prepare a meal.
<small>NATIONAL ARMY MUSEUM 1996-1440</small>

The Gargle Parade. To help fight infections, soldiers of the New Zealand Division were given a mixture to gargle every second day.
<small>NATIONAL ARMY MUSEUM 1996-1440</small>

Brigadier Fulton of the New Zealand Rifle Brigade inspects the footwear and heads of the latest contingent of reinforcements to arrive in France.
<small>RICHARD MILDON</small>

Women, other than nurses, did serve on the Western Front, although in very limited numbers. Those in this photograph have run the canteen at the Lowry Hut for over 18 months. They are, from left to right: Miss Eaton from Wales, Miss Carr from Napier and Miss Russell from Auckland. NATIONAL ARMY MUSEUM 1993-1031 H856

New Zealand press visitors to France in 1918. NATIONAL ARMY MUSEUM 1993-1031 H1006

The popular and effective Corps Commander, Lieutenant General George Harper, addresses New Zealand officers at the end of a field day. The photograph was taken near Bus on 11 May 1918.
NATIONAL ARMY MUSEUM 1993-1031 H581

'Ehoa (I say). How about a fly home now?' read the original annotation. Two Maori soldiers are fascinated by a downed British plane near Bertrancourt. NATIONAL ARMY MUSEUM 1993-1031 H449

As Napoleon is reported to have said, 'An army marches on its stomach'. Good-quality food was essential to the health and morale of an army and the New Zealand Division was no exception. Here, an outdoor cooker is used to prepare food for a Wellington battalion.
NATIONAL ARMY MUSEUM 1999-111 H501

Not all meals cooked were appetising. Here, a group of gunners ceremoniously bury their Christmas dinner. The gunner on the right with the bugle is probably playing the last post.
NATIONAL ARMY MUSEUM 1987-2176

Gallipoli Victoria Cross winner Lieutenant Cyril Bassett at breakfast on 27 August 1918.
NATIONAL ARMY MUSEUM 1993-1031 H979

Meal break at Solesmes, 1918.
NATIONAL ARMY MUSEUM 1999-1711

*New Zealand officers
dine in style in a
captured German trench
on 20 August 1918.
They are sharing the
contents of a parcel that
has just arrived from
New Zealand.*
NATIONAL ARMY MUSEUM
1993-1031 H912

*Gunners of the 3rd Brigade, New
Zealand Field Artillery enjoy dinner at
their first billet in France.*
NATIONAL ARMY MUSEUM 1987-2176

A New Zealand dressing station at Mailly-Maillet on the Somme. Seriously wounded received initial treatment here before being sent to hospitals elsewhere in France and the United Kingdom.
NATIONAL ARMY MUSEUM 1993-1031 H492

New Zealand medical staff and patients in the New Zealand Stationary Hospital at Wisques, near Saint-Omer. The photograph was taken on 17 August 1918.
NATIONAL ARMY MUSEUM 1993-1031 H905

THE POPPINN

The original annotation stated that these were 'some jolly sisters'. But the smiles look a bit strained. New Zealand nurses worked long, hard hours and had to nurse men with horrific injuries. This is the accommodation of the nursing sisters of the New Zealand Stationary Hospital at Wisques. NATIONAL ARMY MUSEUM 1993-1031 H905

A New Zealand doctor examines German prisoners of war on 21 August 1918.
NATIONAL ARMY MUSEUM
1993-1031 H963

'Oh, the pain!' A New Zealand soldier having a tooth extracted.
NATIONAL ARMY MUSEUM
1993-1032 H329

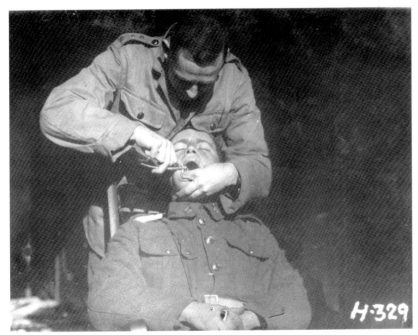

With their band leading, Wellington soldiers march through the ruins of Bapaume.
NATIONAL ARMY MUSEUM
2005-743 H1045

The Otago Regiment Band provides some entertainment at Louvencourt.
NATIONAL ARMY MUSEUM
1999-111 H529

The entertainers. The New Zealand Pierrots and orchestra group put on concerts for the whole New Zealand Division. Their performances were renowned and were given as close to the front as possible.
NATIONAL ARMY MUSEUM
1999-111 H221

'All eyes on the "lady"' stated the original annotation. An open-air concert by the Pierrots given to a neighbouring division but largely attended by New Zealanders. The performance took place at Louvencourt on 7 May 1918.
NATIONAL ARMY MUSEUM
1993-1031 H571

The New Zealand Masonic Association holds a
lodge of instruction at Authie in 1918.
NATIONAL ARMY MUSEUM 1993-1031 H765

This obviously staged photograph does
indicate the importance of fresh reading
material. Newspapers from home and
publications like New Zealand at the Front
were eagerly sought after.
NATIONAL ARMY MUSEUM 1993-1032 H343

Riflemen play a quick hand near Ypres on
19 September 1917.
NATIONAL ARMY MUSEUM 1993-1032 H251

Local 'two-up' schools were in every New
Zealand camp. While gambling was technically
illegal, the authorities tended to turn a blind
eye to this practice. This photograph of the
'Divisional National Game' was taken at
Courcelles in 1918.
NATIONAL ARMY MUSEUM 1994-3346

Maori Pioneers play a game of housie in the field.
NATIONAL ARMY MUSEUM 2005-215 H824

At the New Zealand Division Sports Day at Authie on 23 June 1918, 'Charlie Chaplin' makes ready to enter the bayonet competition. NATIONAL ARMY MUSEUM 1993-1031 H724

A New Zealand officer wins the jumping competition at the New Zealand Divisional Show.
NATIONAL ARMY MUSEUM 1999-1709 H238

*This competitor was
not so lucky.*
RICHARD MILDON H657

The mule steeplechase looks to be very competitive. NATIONAL ARMY MUSEUM 1999-1709 H240

*The winners of the
mule steeplechase.*
RICHARD MILDON H623

A sack race in gas masks cannot have been easy.
RICHARD MILDON H658

Training, instruction in weaponry and inspections were routine for the New Zealanders on the Western Front. Brigadier Herbert Hart inspecting the 3rd Hawkes Bay Platoon of the 3rd Wellington Battalion. NATIONAL ARMY MUSEUM 2004-193 H122

New Zealand soldiers at the Machine Gun School on 25 August 1917 learn about the workings of the Lewis gun.
NATIONAL ARMY MUSEUM 1999-111 H217

New Zealand officers practise with their revolvers on 14 April 1918, prior to moving into the front line. The officer behind the firers does not seem to be sure where the rounds will land.
NATIONAL ARMY MUSEUM
1993-1031 H500

Maori soldiers practise bayonet fighting.
NATIONAL ARMY MUSEUM
2006-512

Pioneers of the Wellington Regiment at work in the transport lines. Carpenters and builders were essential in France.
NATIONAL ARMY MUSEUM
2004-193 H827

Laying duckboards at a New Zealand billet.
<small>NATIONAL ARMY MUSEUM 2002-8</small>

New Zealand engineers repair captured German huts near Bapaume.
<small>NATIONAL ARMY MUSEUM 1992-757 H1200</small>

New Zealand engineers building a bridge in France in 1918. While there appears to be no haste to get this one completed, they could build a bridge like this in less than a day. <small>NATIONAL ARMY MUSEUM 1992-757 H1150</small>

Miscellaneous images

The photographs in this section do not fit easily into a chronological or thematic classification. They include images of various personalities, events and places. They also include photographs of animals, medical treatment, travel and so on. While defying easy classification, they are nonetheless interesting and revealing. They are also part of the rich fabric of experience of New Zealanders during the First World War, and are included for these reasons.

New Zealand troops embarking on HMNZ Troopship No. 35 Willochra. National Army Museum 1986-2086

Troopship No. 49 Maunganui *laden and ready to sail from Wellington.* National Army Museum 1986-2086

Annotated 'Tommy and his kit', this photograph shows soldiers at Lyttelton searching for their kitbags to take on board. This photograph was taken in 1914. By the end of the war New Zealand soldiers did not associate themselves with the British soldier label of 'Tommy'.
National Army Museum 1993-1223

Troops boarding the troopship
SS Remuera. *One presumes the baby is not sailing.*
National Army Museum 1994-3345

*Lifebelt inspection, Wellington
Harbour, prior to sailing.*
NATIONAL ARMY MUSEUM 1993-1223

*Lifeboat drill on board ship, a
routine with which New Zealand
soldiers became all too familiar.*
NATIONAL ARMY MUSEUM 1992-1155

*Lounging on the upper deck. There
was considerable free time on board
the troopships.*
NATIONAL ARMY MUSEUM 1992-1155

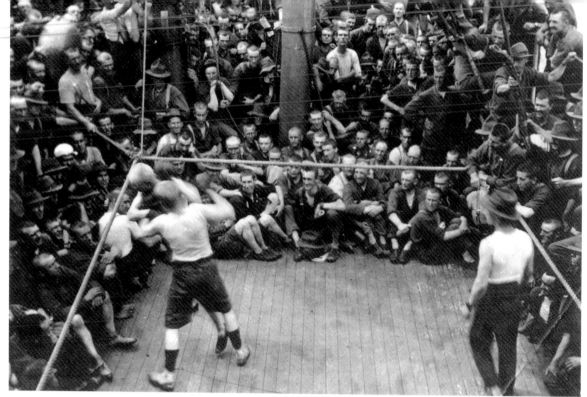

Entertainment was a feature of the long voyage to the United Kingdom. This boxing match on a troopship has drawn a large audience. NATIONAL ARMY MUSEUM 1990-409

The traditional 'King Neptune' ceremony that takes place when a vessel crosses the equator was a standard ritual on troopships and provided plenty of amusement. NATIONAL ARMY MUSEUM 1993-1223

The New Zealand Engineer Troop practises a haka. The Field Troop eventually won the haka competition on this ship. NATIONAL ARMY MUSEUM 1992-763, NATIONAL ARMY MUSEUM 1992-763

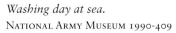

A Sunday church service on board a troopship. NATIONAL ARMY MUSEUM 1990-1717

Washing day at sea. NATIONAL ARMY MUSEUM 1990-409

Onboard entertainment draws a crowd. NATIONAL ARMY MUSEUM 1993-1223

The original annotation stated that this was 'a New Zealander's defiant expression on arriving in England to fight the Germans'. It is quite a captivating image, but the defiant expression could also have been aimed at the English.

NATIONAL ARMY MUSEUM 1986-2086

This British plane wreck is the result of an accident rather than aerial dog-fighting. Wrecked aircraft held a peculiar fascination for New Zealand soldiers. National Army Museum 1993-1293

A group of New Zealand pilots who are training at a civilian flying school at Acton. The pilot on the left is Hew Montgomerie. The others, from the left (surnames only), are Holmes, Culver and Melville. Susanna Norris

Soldiers in gas masks have an eerie quality when photographed up close.
NATIONAL ARMY MUSEUM
1992-763

Not all New Zealand war service was done in uniform. Roger Montgomerie was a forestry expert who spent the war years in the United Kingdom directing logging operations. These logs are destined to become pit props in the trenches of the Western Front. SUSANNA NORRIS

Not all of the 10,000 horses that left New Zealand during the war years survived the voyage. Here, a dead horse that sailed with the Main Body is unceremoniously dumped overboard.
NATIONAL ARMY MUSEUM 1990-1712

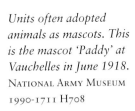

Units often adopted animals as mascots. This is the mascot 'Paddy' at Vauchelles in June 1918.
NATIONAL ARMY MUSEUM 1990-1711 H708

Moses, an Egyptian donkey and mascot of the New Zealand Army Service Corps, looks to be quite a handful when 'in a playful mood'.
NATIONAL ARMY MUSEUM
1999-111 H527

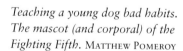

Teaching a young dog bad habits. The mascot (and corporal) of the Fighting Fifth. MATTHEW POMEROY

Jimmy, the mascot of the Otago Mounted Rifles. Jimmy also learned some bad habits, including drinking beer from a tin. PAULINE WILKINSON

The champions of the Divisional Dog Show. Doreen Parry

Another pet. A desert fox and an Auckland Mounted Rifles trooper. National Army Museum 1996-946

A win-win situation. New Zealand medics milk a cow abandoned by its owners during the German advance in 1918. This photograph was taken on 1 April 1918. National Army Museum 1999-111 H462

Saunders, Foote and Fyson out in the cold of Sling Camp, Bulford, and not looking too happy to be there. NATIONAL ARMY MUSEUM 2000-500

Mealtime at the New Zealand Rifle Brigade Officers Mess, Matruh, Egypt. NATIONAL ARMY MUSEUM 1990-409

A snack on the railway tracks near Alexandria for officers of the New Zealand Rifle Brigade. The order is not clear, but they are named as Puttick, Purdy, Lankshear, Gilbert and McAlister. NATIONAL ARMY MUSEUM 1990-409

'Next, please!' Rifleman C.K. Gasquoine receives a rough haircut from his friend Buck in the desert near Matruh. NATIONAL ARMY MUSEUM 1990-409

Two 'Main Body' men. Captain Shepherd on the left and Captain Frederick Starnes on the right, both of the 2nd Canterbury Battalion. During the battle of the Somme in 1916, Starnes displayed outstanding leadership and gallantry and was recommended for the Victoria Cross. General Russell did not think that officers should receive the VC and awarded an immediate DSO instead.
MATTHEW POMEROY

The 'Wild Man' of the New Zealand Division. John Douglas Stark, or 'Starkie' as he was known, became notorious throughout the New Zealand Division. His reckless courage earned him recommendations for gallantry awards, which were cancelled because of his lack of military discipline and troublemaking when out of the line. Among his exploits were an escape from the infamous Le Havre military prison, and rescuing from certain death the future New Zealand Prime Minister, Gordon Coates. The New Zealand author Robin Hyde later wrote two books about Starkie, which greatly embellished his deeds. Starkie is on the left, with Sergeant Quinell in the middle and an unidentified soldier to the right.
NATIONAL ARMY MUSEUM 2007-27

Captain Hunt and Sergeant Quinell after a shipboard inoculation.
NATIONAL ARMY MUSEUM 2007-27

Recording events for posterity. Officially, cameras were forbidden, but many soldiers used them. This book would not have been possible if they hadn't.
NATIONAL ARMY MUSEUM 2007-27

Some of the 'big men' of New Zealand's war effort. Sir Joseph Ward and William Massey, on either side of Field Marshal Sir Douglas Haig. The officer on the left is Brigadier G.S. Richardson, the officer in charge of the New Zealand Headquarters in London. NATIONAL ARMY MUSEUM 1991-321

A group of New Zealand soldiers 'somewhere in France'. The soldier on the left, front row, is Herbert George Wilson. K.M. TEMPLETON

Sergeant Samuel Forsyth won the VC in the battle of Bapaume in 1918. Unfortunately, it was a posthumous award.
NATIONAL ARMY MUSEUM 1992-757

A short spell for these New Zealand soldiers before the never-ending task of digging resumes. JEAN DALES

Two more VC winners. Sergeant Samuel Frickleton (left) and the newly commissioned Leslie W. Andrew. JEAN DALES

299

*'A picturesque
Mediterranean sunset'.
The photograph was
taken from a hospital
ship early in 1916.*
NATIONAL ARMY MUSEUM
1986-1753

HMS Albion *aground at the Dardanelles.* NATIONAL ARMY MUSEUM 1991-585

Naval vessels steering a zigzag course to avoid being easy prey for German submarines.
NATIONAL ARMY MUSEUM 1991-321 A6

New Zealand's contribution to British sea power and to the arms race of the early twentieth century. The battle cruiser HMS New Zealand *in 1919.* ROYAL NEW ZEALAND NAVY MUSEUM ABT0068

HMS New Zealand *fought in the one big surface fleet battle of the war at Jutland in 1916. She was slightly damaged by German naval gunfire. Here the crew hoists a piece of shell shrapnel that hit the ship. It weighed some 500 kilograms and is now at the Royal New Zealand Navy Museum in Auckland.*
ROYAL NEW ZEALAND NAVY MUSEUM ABT0141

The SS Marquette *was used as a transport ship during the war. She sailed from Alexandria on 19 February 1915 loaded with troops, war matériel, 500 mules and the No. 1 Stationary Hospital. The vessel was torpedoed on 23 October and sank with a huge loss of life, including 10 New Zealand nurses.*
NATIONAL ARMY MUSEUM 1986-1753

Some of the fortunate Marquette *survivors ready to go ashore at Salonika.*
NATIONAL ARMY MUSEUM 1986-1753

The 2nd Contingent of New Zealand Nurses photographed immediately before leaving New Zealand in May 1915. Matron Marie Cameron is in the centre of the front row. Matron Cameron was seriously injured when the Marquette *sank and her health never recovered.* NATIONAL ARMY MUSEUM 1986-1753

New Zealand nurses on the steps of the 17th British General Hospital, Alexandria.
NATIONAL ARMY MUSEUM 1986-1753

The hospital ship Maheno, *which together with her sister ship* Marama *made 17 voyages to New Zealand during the war, bringing some 47,000 wounded and sick New Zealand soldiers home.*
NATIONAL ARMY MUSEUM 1999-3208

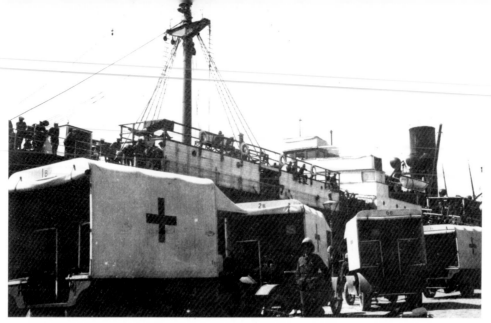

Ambulance lorries being loaded on to a hospital ship.
National Army Museum 1991-587

Mechanics service the Division's vehicles at the 'cars' hospital' in France. National Army Museum 2005-215 H189

A ward in a British ambulance train in France. This was how the seriously wounded, including New Zealanders, reached hospitals in the United Kingdom. National Army Museum 1991-321 A11

A wounded New Zealander arrives at the No. 1 New Zealand General Hospital at Brockenhurst.
NATIONAL ARMY MUSEUM 1992-750

Brockenhurst, Hampshire, 14 miles from Southampton and in the woodlands of the New Forest, was a perfect setting for a large military hospital. There were two other New Zealand military hospitals in the United Kingdom — at Walton-on-Thames and Codford. Neither of these could match the beautiful setting of Brockenhurst, which became the main New Zealand military hospital of the war. NATIONAL ARMY MUSEUM 1992-750

Nurses and patients relax in Brockenhurst's lovely gardens. NATIONAL ARMY MUSEUM 1992-750

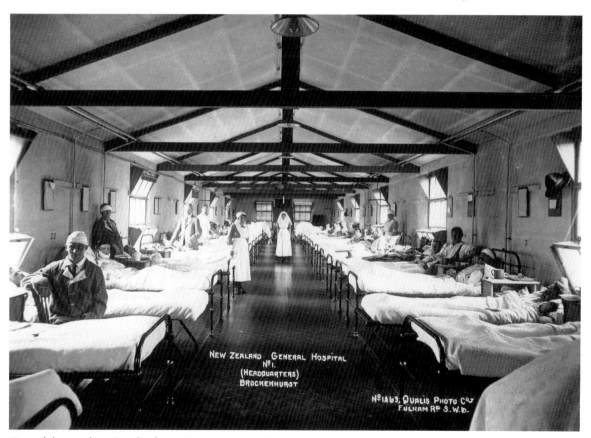

One of the wards at Brockenhurst. NATIONAL ARMY MUSEUM 1992-750

Patients receiving treatment at Brockenhurst.
NATIONAL ARMY MUSEUM 1992-750

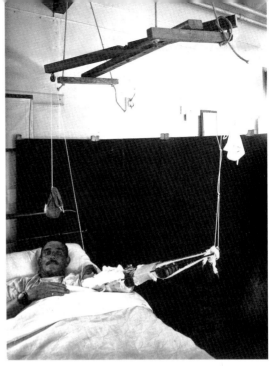

A patient at Brockenhurst suffering from an arm injury. NATIONAL ARMY MUSEUM 1992-750

A photograph of New Zealand nurses. Some 550 New Zealand nurses served with the New Zealand Expeditionary Force during the war. Most people assumed they had been off on a 'great adventure', which was far from the truth. They received very little support upon their return to New Zealand and many never recovered from their war experiences. NATIONAL ARMY MUSEUM 1990-1717

Wounded soldiers relaxing in one of the lounges at Brockenhurst.
NATIONAL ARMY MUSEUM
1992-750

The dining room at Brockenhurst, ready to receive the patients able to walk to their meals.
NATIONAL ARMY MUSEUM
1992-750

The snooker lounge at Brockenhurst.
NATIONAL ARMY MUSEUM
1992-750

Some wounded New Zealanders enjoy the sun outdoors.
NATIONAL ARMY MUSEUM
1990-1717

Nurses and soldiers pose at a bomb shelter.
NATIONAL ARMY MUSEUM 1990-1717

Wounded soldiers and nurses on a picnic in the Brockenhurst grounds in 1918.
NATIONAL ARMY MUSEUM
1992-1155

Ward 19, Brockenhurst, on Christmas Day, 1916.
NATIONAL ARMY MUSEUM 1986-1753

Nurses relax at the Kia Toa Club, Torquay. Such opportunities were rare for the New Zealand nurses.
NATIONAL ARMY MUSEUM 1992-750

A dusting of snow decorates Brockenhurst. The photograph was taken in March 1917.
NATIONAL ARMY MUSEUM 1986-1753

Not all New Zealanders left Brockenhurst. These two photographs are of New Zealanders' graves in the grounds of the hospital.

Immediately after the Armistice, General Russell set up a comprehensive education scheme for members of the New Zealand Expeditionary Force. Many soldiers took advantage of the scheme to fill in the months awaiting passage back to New Zealand. These men are attending a class in the United Kingdom.
NATIONAL ARMY MUSEUM 1994-3345

A class in water-divining at Hornchurch, given as part of the YMCA educational scheme.
NATIONAL ARMY MUSEUM 1994-3345

New Zealand during the war

For an event widely acknowledged as the most traumatic in New Zealand's history, historians have tended to underestimate the impact of the First World War on the country. New Zealand, with a population of barely a million people, gave so much to the war effort, and the strains and tensions created during the war years were long-lasting and deeply felt. The intense sadness, even bitterness, associated with the human cost of the war also lingered long after the final shots were fired.

For the first time in its history New Zealand sent a vast army to war. More than 102,000 men embarked for service overseas; about 10 per cent of the total population. This was over 40 per cent of all men of military age and 20 per cent of all eligible manpower. Having this number of men away for so long placed enormous pressures on those who remained. This was felt in all spheres: economic, social, political and religious. The worry of mothers, fathers, siblings and other relatives for those at the sharp end should not be underestimated, either.

This concern, when combined with the diet of imperial patriotism fed to New Zealanders over the years, produced a society that became militaristic and intolerant. Conformity to the war effort was demanded, dissent was greeted with hostility and punitive action. Those suspected of shirking their duties or of being disloyal encountered intense resentment. White Feather Leagues roamed the streets looking for young men they suspected of avoiding their war duties. Businesses with German names suffered vandalism and a downturn in trade. In Christchurch, the bells of the Lutheran Church were smashed. No other warring nation treated its conscientious objectors as harshly as New Zealand. Indeed, so extreme was the response in this country that conscientious objectors were deprived of the right to vote for 10 years, and 14 of them were even shipped to Europe for forced service on the Western Front. Such actions indicate that the springs of society were wound very tight.

If New Zealand, with a few exceptions, wholeheartedly embraced the war effort, women were essential to creating and maintaining this support. Not only did New Zealand women 'keep the home fires burning', they had a host of other duties, too. No one has counted the number of knitted garments sent to New Zealand soldiers, but they must number in the millions. The comfort parcels sent to soldiers reached similar levels. Women entered the workforce and joined voluntary organisations to assist the war effort. Mothers with young children struggled to find ways to pay the bills on a soldier's allotment and raise their children, whose father might be absent for years. 'Three children to keep on a private's pay' was the recurring thought of Augusta in Robin Hyde's novel *The Godwits Fly*. Augusta did survive and rediscovered her own strength in doing so, but it was never easy. It was never easy for the women — whether mother, wife, sister, fiancée — the New Zealand soldiers had left behind.

The cost of New Zealand's massive war effort was reflected in the heavy casualty toll. Nearly 60,000 of those men who embarked overseas became casualties, with 18,166 dying while in uniform. These are only the physical manifestations of war damage; the hidden scars were also numerous and enduring. If physical evidence of the terrible cost was needed, in every city, town, village and district of New Zealand, war memorials were erected to those killed. No community was spared this sacrifice; every person in

New Zealand either had a close relative or friend killed or maimed, or knew people so affected. In some small towns today, there are more names on the memorials than people still living there. The casualty list for the First World War remains New Zealand's largest ever and exceeds all the other wars of the twentieth century combined. It is impossible to overstate the depth of trauma, bitterness and loss caused by the First World War. As one historian quoted by Michael King so eloquently expressed it: 'the new generation [of New Zealanders] did not need to be told that the angel of death had passed over the land: they had heard the beating of its wings'.

New Zealand continued to produce thousands of partially trained soldiers throughout the war and introduced conscription in August 1916 to ensure the steady flow of men was maintained. As well as the Main Body, 42 Reinforcements Drafts, each around 2000 men, left New Zealand for the war. A large crowd sees off men destined for the 18th Reinforcements, as they leave Nelson on 27 June 1916. TED SCOTT

New Zealand soldiers in camp. The tall man with his arms spread is 35-year-old Private Archibald Robertson, who was 6 feet 6 inches, or 1.98 metres. No one believed that someone that tall would survive in the trenches of France but he did. JANET WITHERS

D Company of the 17th Reinforcements march over the Rimutakas in September 1916.
NATIONAL ARMY MUSEUM
1999-3208

Mounted Riflemen of the 35th Reinforcements provide the Wellington Town Piquet.
NATIONAL ARMY MUSEUM
1987-1733

Members of B Company of the 23rd Reinforcements air their bedding at a training camp. Blankets and greatcoats are all neatly folded and the kitbags are in neat lines.
MATTHEW POMEROY

Men of the 18th Reinforcements marching out from Featherston Camp. They were to march over the Rimutaka Ranges to reach Trentham Camp by nightfall. NATIONAL ARMY MUSEUM 2007-382

Soldiers practise with the Vickers heavy machine gun. FRANCES DAVEY

More machine-gun practice. The soldier on the right is Robert Tilsley, a Gallipoli veteran who served in both World Wars. FRANCES DAVEY

*New Zealand
soldiers coaling a
vessel, probably in
Wellington Harbour.*
MARK FEBERY

*Conveyor belt to the
war. Two troopships,
the* Tahiti *on the left
and the* Athenic *on
the right, lie ready in
Lyttelton Harbour to
receive their human
cargo.*
NATIONAL ARMY
MUSEUM 1992-742

*And still they go.
More troops embark
at Lyttelton.*
NATIONAL ARMY
MUSEUM 1993-1223

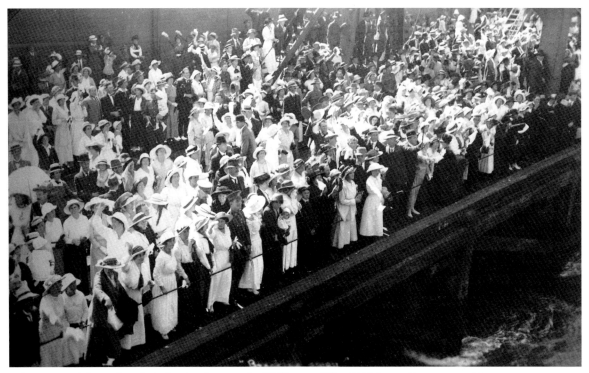

A large crowd dressed in their Sunday best on the Wellington Wharf bid farewell to a troopship.
NATIONAL ARMY MUSEUM 1990-1717

Part of 'England's Unlimited Empire Resources', so the original annotation read. Another contingent of New Zealand soldiers disembarks in the United Kingdom in 1917. NATIONAL ARMY MUSEUM 1986-2086

After the landing at Gallipoli, New Zealanders became used to the sight of wounded soldiers. This is the home of Sir Francis Henry Dillon Bell, a leading lawyer, Member of Parliament and future New Zealand Prime Minister, albeit for a few short months. During the war years it was used as the Taumaru Military Convalescent Hospital. The beautiful, spacious home was situated at Lowry Bay, Wellington. National Army Museum 1987-1228

Recuperating soldiers play a game of cricket in the grounds of the Bell residence. National Army Museum 1987-1228

'When the Daimler would not go', reads the annotation, the nurses and soldiers of the Taumaru Military Convalescent Hospital went out to give it a push. The horse was also of great assistance. National Army Museum 1987-1228

Some convalescing soldiers off for a row at Lowry Bay. NATIONAL ARMY MUSEUM 1987-1228

Most New Zealanders wholeheartedly supported the war effort of New Zealand, despite its mounting cost. New Zealand women were enthusiastic supporters of the cause in the early months of the war. Dressing up in a soldier's uniform was a way of showing support. MATTHEW POMEROY

No. 12 REINFORCEMENTS.
CANDIDATE.

DOROTHY WRIGHT

Greetings and Good Wishes from the Hutt Valley Rosebud Carnival.

Dorothy Wright shows her support for the men of the 12th Reinforcements. MATTHEW POMEROY

A hairdressing competition in Wellington raises money for the Red Cross fund. NATIONAL ARMY MUSEUM 1986-2086

Young men of Dunedin demonstrate their loyalty to the cause and indicate what they think the fate of the Kaiser should be. This photograph was taken after the Armistice. NGAIRE YOUNG

Children were also drawn into the war effort. These children are part of a fundraising effort for the war. MARK FEBERY

Children used in a display of patriotism and Empire support. Some of them do not look too pleased to be there. The historian James Belich has recorded how one little girl, sick of hearing about the plight of 'poor little Belgium', found herself in deep disgrace for shouting: 'Damn the little Belgians'. Some of the children in this image look as if they could be thinking something similar. MARK FEBERY

Brighty (Dorothy) Craw raffles her pony for the New Zealand war effort. HERBERT RIX

Children from the Kaniere state school on the way to Hokitika to take part in Armistice Day celebrations. THE WEST COAST HISTORICAL MUSEUM, HOKITIKA

The children pose on the steps of the Carnegie Library at Hokitika. They are dressed to represent the victorious Allies.

BACK ROW, LEFT TO RIGHT: *Bill Wells (France), Fred Selby (soldier), Una Borrows (Belgium), Nora Chesterman (Scotland), Isabel Forsyth (Red Cross nurse), Dorrie Howat (Britannia), Miss Charlotte Wylie (pupil teacher, USA), Eileen Pfahlert (Ireland), Clara Morris (nurse).*
MIDDLE ROW: *Millie Manson (Holland), Mihaka Parker (Maori), Elizabeth Cummings (USA?), Marion Hackle (Eire), Cathie Manson (Peace), Lou Milner (Holland).*
FRONT ROW: *Peg Wells (New Zealand), Sybil Newman (nurse), Olive Chesterman (Belgium), Frances Wells (nurse), Connie Newman (nurse), Harriet Selby (England?).*

Epilogue: the cost

Anyone who doubts that the war was a traumatic experience for New Zealand need only look at the following section of photographs. As historians Jay Winter and Blaine Baggett have commented: 'War is always the destroyer of families and the Great War was to date the greatest destroyer of them all.' This was certainly true for New Zealand.

The casualties of the First World War were not limited to the dead and wounded. They also included those men who returned, even if many of them seemed unaffected by what they had seen and done. In truth, most of the men who returned from this war were casualties who had to live with their war memories for the rest of their lives. For many, the war actually came to dominate their lives. As one participant in the Passchendaele battles told leading British historian Lyn Macdonald: 'In a way, I lived my whole life between the ages of nineteen and twenty-three. Everything that happened after that was almost an anti-climax.'

The last word here is from a famous American writer who was no stranger to war. In the words of Ernest Hemingway: 'Never think that war, no matter how necessary, nor how justified, is not a crime.'

Warning: The photographs that follow contain images that should disturb.

Wounded soldiers at the Kia Ora Club, Brockenhurst. National Army Museum 1992-750

Firing party for a soldier who died of his wounds.
National Army Museum 1990-1717

The last post is played for the same soldier.
National Army Museum 1990-1717

Wounded soldiers receiving treatment at Brockenhurst. NATIONAL ARMY MUSEUM 1992-750

Dental technicians work to replace teeth and jaws smashed by shell-fire.
NATIONAL ARMY MUSEUM 1992-750

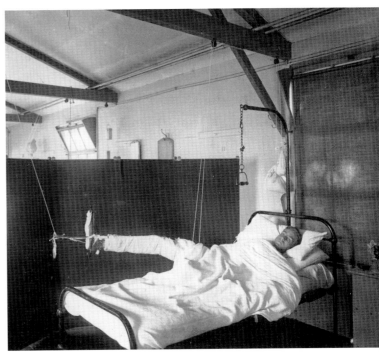

A soldier with a leg injury in traction at Brockenhurst.
NATIONAL ARMY MUSEUM 1992-750

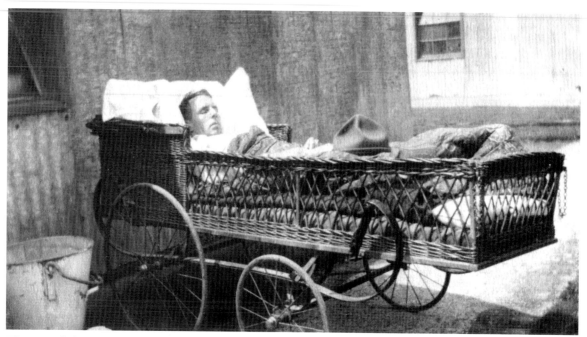

The wounded Sergeant Dillon takes a nap in the sun at Brockenhurst. NATIONAL ARMY MUSEUM 1992-1156

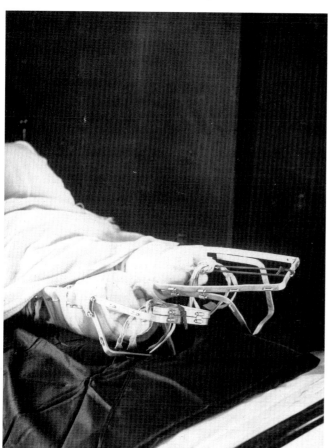

Double amputee at Brockenhurst.
NATIONAL ARMY MUSEUM 1992-750

Flying shell fragments caused horrific injuries to soldiers. The following images show some of the damage caused. They also show the remarkable repair work done by surgeons, including the New Zealand surgeon Captain S.D. Rhind, MBChB. The first two wounded soldiers were Captain Rhind's patients. The pain from these injuries and the medical treatment that followed is unimaginable, but the courage of those being treated is clearly evident.
GILL MARTIN

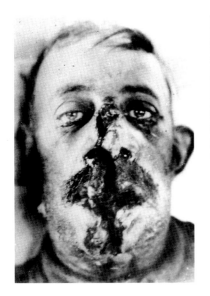

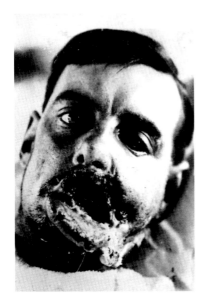
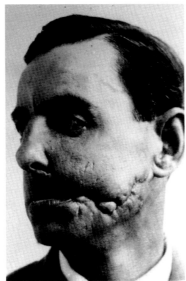
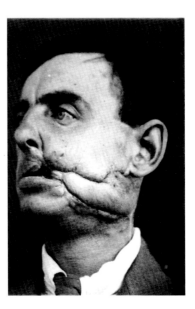

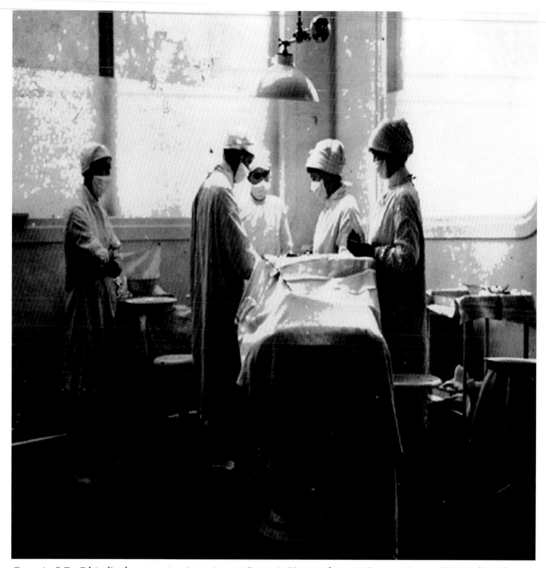

Captain S.D. Rhind's theatre team in action at Queen's Hospital (now Queen Mary's Hospital), Sidcup, Kent. GILL MARTIN

The images on the following three pages are from the Gillies Archives, Queen Mary's Hospital, Sidcup, Kent. The archives are named after the gifted New Zealand-born surgeon Sir Harold Gillies, who was the hospital's leading practitioner of maxiofacial surgery. Queen Mary's Hospital is really the birthplace of modern plastic surgery. What is amazing is that the operations were performed without sulphur drugs, plasma or penicillin.

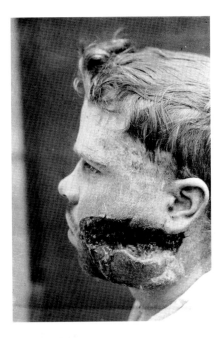

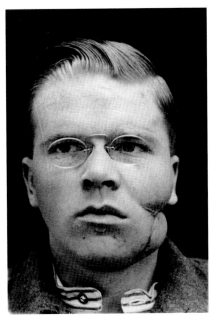

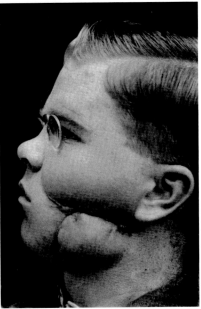

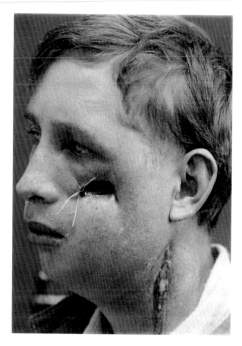

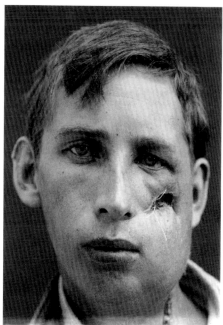

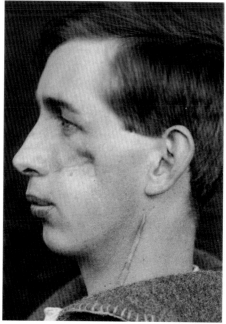

With the permission of the Curator, Gillies Archives, Frognal Centre for Medical Studies, Queen Mary's Hospital, Sidcup, United Kingdom

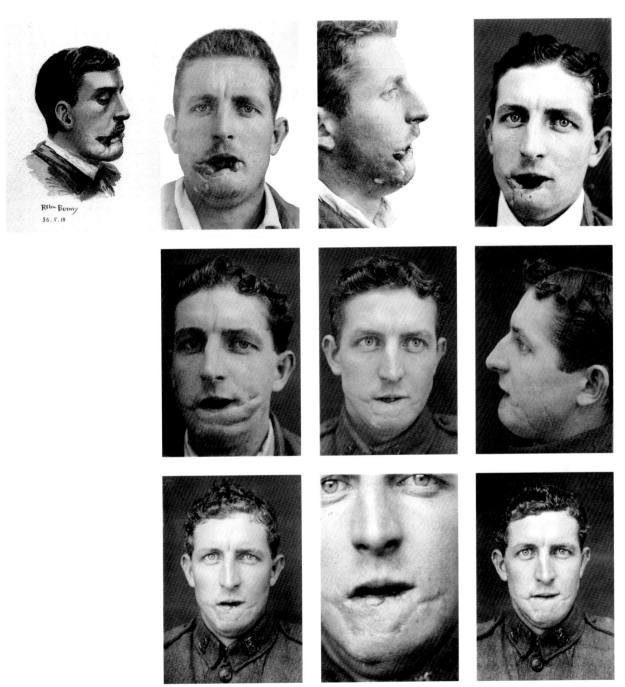

WITH THE PERMISSION OF THE CURATOR, GILLIES ARCHIVES, FROGNAL CENTRE FOR MEDICAL STUDIES, QUEEN MARY'S HOSPITAL, SIDCUP, UNITED KINGDOM

GV RI

HE whom this scroll commemorates was numbered among those who, at the call of King and Country, left all that was dear to them, endured hardness, faced danger, and finally passed out of the sight of men by the path of duty and self-sacrifice, giving up their own lives that others might live in freedom.

Let those who come after see to it that his name be not forgotten.

Trooper George Wyse Smith
Canterbury Mtd. Rifles, N.Z.E.F.

Pretty, but no consolation for losing a loved one. During the war the sense of sacrifice and debt was profound. It has become diluted over the years, but we do remember them. NEIL BRUERE

Select bibliography

Duncan Anderson, *Glass Warriors. The Camera at War*, Collins, London, 2005.

C.E.W. Bean and H.S. Gullett, *Official History of Australia in the War of 1914–18 Vol XII Photographic Record of the War*, Angus & Robertson Ltd, Sydney, 1923.

Joan Beaumont, *Australian Defence: Sources and Statistics*, Oxford University Press, Melbourne, 2001.

James Belich, *Paradise Reforged. A history of the New Zealanders from the 1880s to the year 2000*, Allen Lane, The Penguin Press, Auckland, 2001.

Ormond Burton, *The Silent Division*, Angus & Robertson, Sydney, 1935.

Sandy Callister, *War, Seen Through Photographs, Darkly; the photographic representation of World War One from a New Zealand perspective*, Doctor of Philosophy thesis, University of Auckland, 2005.

Sandy Callister, *The Face of War. New Zealand's Great War Photography*, Auckland University Press, Auckland, 2008.

Les Carlyon, *Gallipoli*, Pan Macmillan Australia, Sydney, 2001.

Les Carlyon, *The Great War*, Pan Macmillan Australia, Sydney, 2006.

John Crawford (ed.), *No Better Death. The Great War diaries and letters of William G. Malone*, Reed Books, Auckland, 2005.

John Crawford and Ian McGibbon (eds), *New Zealand's Great War. New Zealand, the Allies and the First World War*, Exisle Publishing, Auckland, 2007.

The Fairfax Library in association with Daniel O'Keefe, *Hurley at War. The Photography and Diaries of Frank Hurley in Two World Wars*, John Fairfax & Sons Ltd, Sydney, 1986.

Glyn Harper (ed.), *Letters from the Battlefield. New Zealand soldiers write home. 1914–1918*, HarperCollins Publishers, Auckland, 2001.

Glyn Harper, *Dark Journey. Three key New Zealand battles of the Western Front*, HarperCollins Publishers, Auckland, 2007.

Richard Holmes, *The First World War in Photographs*, Carlton Books, London, 2001.

Richard Holmes, *Tommy. The British Soldier on the Western Front 1914–1918*, Harper Perennial, London, 2005.

Peter Howe, *Shooting Under Fire. The World of the War Photographer*, Artisan, New York, 2002.

Greg Kerr, *Private Wars. Personal Records of the Anzacs in the Great War*, Oxford University Press, Melbourne, 2000.

Michael King, *New Zealanders at War*, Heinemann Publishers, Auckland, 1981.

Michael King, *The Penguin History of New Zealand*, Viking, Auckland, 2003.

Terry Kinloch, *Devils on Horses. In the Words of the Anzacs in the Middle East 1916–19*, Exisle Publishing, Auckland, 2007.

Phillip Knightley, *The Eye of War. Words and Photographs from the Front Line*, Smithsonian Books, Washington, D.C., n.d.

Andrew Macdonald, *On My Way to the Somme. New Zealanders and the bloody offensive of 1916*, HarperCollins Publishers, Auckland, 2005.

Ian McGibbon (ed.), *The Oxford Companion to New Zealand Military History*, Oxford University Press, Auckland, 2000.

Ian McGibbon (ed.), *New Zealand Battlefields and Memorials of the Western Front*, Oxford University Press, Auckland, 2001.

Reginald Pound, *Gillies. Surgeon Extraordinary*, Michael Joseph, London, 1964.

Christopher Pugsley, *Gallipoli. The New Zealand Story*, Sceptre Auckland, 1990.

Christopher Pugsley, *On the Fringe of Hell. New Zealanders and military discipline in the First World War*, Hodder & Stoughton, Auckland, 1991.

Richard Stowers, *Bloody Gallipoli. the New Zealanders' Story*, David Bateman, Auckland, 2005.

Tim Travers, *Gallipoli 1915*, Tempus Publishing Ltd, Brimscombe Port Stroud, 2002.

Paul Whittle (ed.), *World War I in Photographs*, Eagle Editions Ltd, Royston, Hertfordshire, 2003.